Living an Alcohol-free Life

YOUR Way

MARY STUART

Copyright © Mary Stuart, First Published 2021

ISBN 978-0-6451321-0-6

All Rights Reserved. No part of this book may be reproduced or used in any manner without the prior written permission of the copyright owner.

The adoption and application of the information in this book is at the discretion of the reader and is his or her sole responsibility.

Edited by: Sarah Phillips and Karen Crombie

Book Cover Design: Jenn Rackham

Author photograph: Mark Strachan

To Paul, you are my love, my rock and I could not have done this without your love and support. My life is so much better with you in it. To our fur baby Eddie, who makes me smile every day.

To my beautiful mama, I miss you every day and wish I could have at least five more minutes with you.

To Dale, Dean and Simone, I love you.

Emma Franklin Bell, Jemima Carroll, Jenn Rackham, Karen Crombie, David Lawton and Sarah Phillips for your wonderful guidance and most of all patience in the process of writing this book.

Note of Caution

This book is not intended to replace the support of a psychologist, psychiatrist or any other health professional. If you are physically dependent on alcohol, it is not safe for you to quit drinking without the support of an appropriately qualified professional.
Also, if any of the stories in this book trigger you in any way, please consult a health professional.

Contents

Introduction		11
Chapter 1	FEAR AND CATASTROPHISING	15
Chapter 2	INSECURITIES	25
Chapter 3	DRINKING 'FRIENDS'	35
Chapter 4	BEING SOMEONE YOU ARE NOT	45
Chapter 5	TELLING OTHERS	55
Chapter 6	GOING OUT, WITHOUT A PLAN	63
Chapter 7	ANTIDEPRESSANTS AND COUNSELLING	71
Chapter 8	DATING AND RELATIONSHIPS	81
Chapter 9	WHEN DRINKING STARTS TO AFFECT WORK	91
Chapter 10	SECOND ATTEMPT... OR WAS IT?	101
Chapter 11	ALCOHOL AND DISEASE	111
Chapter 12	CELEBRATIONS AND STRESSFUL EVENTS	119
Chapter 13	LIVING AN ALCOHOL-FREE LIFE	129
Chapter 14	STAYING ON TRACK (EVEN WHEN LIFE THROWS THINGS AT YOU)	139
Final Message		149
References		151

Introduction

Living an alcohol-free life was always something I yearned to achieve, however I did not quite know WHY I had that desire. Yes, I wanted to be healthier, fitter and not feel so lousy every morning, however, going alcohol-free always seemed so scary and out of my reach. I always thought going to parties would be a blast if I was drinking or drowning my sorrows when I was sad, always believing drinking would just make everything better.

It didn't make things better, at all.

Alcohol is poison, there is no doubt about it. The World Health Organisation (WHO)[1] states it has a toxic effect on your whole body, and also contributes globally to three million deaths a year. Although the report states that males are affected more than women, based on what

---

1. https://www.who.int/news-room/fact-sheets/detail/alcohol

I have experienced, there are more and more people in general, who drink to excess and are not willing to admit they have a drinking problem.

You may have bought this book because you want to quit drinking altogether, because having those few drinks every night makes you feel uncomfortable or you are feeling like I was, where you couldn't take your foot off the accelerator. Or maybe you simply want to know how I now live an alcohol-free life. Whatever the reason, I'm sure you have more than a passing interest in quitting drinking, plus I have a sneaking suspicion you have already bought or downloaded several books on the subject of alcohol-free living. There are many ways to live an alcohol-free life. I and others are testament to that, people such as: Rob Lowe, Russell Brand, Kelly Osbourne and Elton John. These are only just a few who have invested in their alcohol-free life and did it *their way*. The reason for writing this book is for you to do the same.

By being a part of alcohol-free Facebook group pages and reading so many alcohol-free books, I've realised there were many people going through a similar experience and feeling exactly the same way I was. I knew there were and are many people who want to help themselves, just like I did. This book is about self-discovery and for you to ask questions as to why this relates specifically to you and will allow you to live an alcohol-free life, *YOUR* way.

Quitting drinking is not as easy as it might seem, especially if you choose to just stop without understanding why you drink. When you talk to someone who has been living an alcohol-free life for a significant amount of time, you may simply be in awe of them and think, *'I would love to do that too'*, never really giving it another thought, then continue to drink. It takes a certain mindset and dedication to do this, and at first it can seem daunting. It can seem so daunting that most people who want to stop drinking, don't ever actually do it. This is such a shame, because everyone should be able to invest in an alcohol-free life if they choose to.

Each time I have tried to quit drinking, I learned more about what works for me and what I feel are my key ingredients to making it worth the effort. Along the way I have made a lot of mistakes; many mornings I have woken up and wondered why I was still drinking. I want you to have the information to be able to change your thinking in regard to alcohol and the associations you have with it. Finding your path will be the key to changing your view of drinking alcohol.

When I decided to write this book, I put together what I had learned so you can avoid some of the mistakes I made. I do, however, want *you* to discover what works for *you*. This book will not only make the process easier and less stressful, but also give you some ways of thinking about *why you* drink and *how you* can change *your* mindset and behaviour. I believe deciding to stop drinking is much more than just quitting. Based on my experiences, getting your headspace right is key to quitting drinking and the more you know about *why* you drink and the associations you have to it, the more likely you are to feel confident, clear, and focused when *you* finally decide to live an alcohol-free life.

Each chapter in this book covers a little of my story, the process of learning why I drank, and some questions to ask yourself, about your own drinking. At the end of each chapter there are two sections. Firstly, *Mary's wisdom for living an alcohol-free life*, which outline things I learned along the way and which may help you. These are not intended to tell you what to do – it simply demonstrates what I learned which may help you along your journey. Secondly, I have added *Journal Prompt* questions for you to answer, which will give you a lot of information to help you be clearer about why you want to quit drinking. I highly recommend you use a journal (or the journal pages at the end of each chapter) to assist you in answering these questions. Keep it as your reference journal where you record your thoughts and ideas, or any other bits and pieces related to your drinking.

Of course, it is best to read this book from start to finish, but you are also able to go directly to the sections which apply to you, if that suits you better. No matter how you choose to approach this book, keeping the journal is very important for you to reflect on, as this will give you the power to continue. Just remember, the journal is not there to write and leave, it is there to write and read. Going back over what you have written is key to building up your alcohol-free muscle.

You may have quit many times, just like me and now you want to take the leap, move to the next level, and to live an alcohol-free life for good. I want to help you change your association to alcohol and the impact it is having on your life.

You have made the decision to buy this book, now let me help you to live an alcohol-free life, **YOUR** way!

Let's get to it!

Mary x
marystuart.net.au

Chapter 1
Fear and Catastrophising

'People often laughed at me and I, in my drunken haze, would look around a room and could barely open my eyelids. It always felt like all eyes were on me.'
Mary Stuart

I remember to this day, my first taste of alcohol. It was a hot Australian summer day, and we were with family and friends enjoying a BBQ in the backyard of our home. I was around ten years old and remember watching the grown-ups around a table drinking, happily chatting, laughing, and watching the children running around in the sun. We would often get sunburnt from head to toe and at the end of the day mum would liberally rub calamine lotion all over us when we came inside, as sunscreen was not really used all that often when I was a child.

My mum was cradling a purple and silver can of vodka and passionfruit in her lap and as she went to take a sip, I softly tapped her on the shoulder to ask if I could sit on her lap. As I clumsily crawled up, I cupped my hands over her ear and quietly whispered, *'Can I please have some of your drink?'* She turned to me and said in a stern voice, *'No, Mary, that drink is for grown-ups.'* As the adults around the table turned to look at me, I remember my cheeks blushing and shyly pushing my face into my mum's shoulder. I then whispered, *'Please can I just have a taste?'* I kept pestering her, over and over again to just give me a small taste. All of a sudden she gave in and said, *'Just a little taste and please do not ask me again.'* I grabbed Mum's (what seemed to be) huge vodka and passionfruit can with both small hands as she cradled it underneath, to ensure I only had the little taste she promised. She then quickly pulled it from my lips and sternly said, *'That's enough, you've had enough!'*

Growing up in Australia in the 1970s and '80s, many parents drank alcohol to excess and smoked cigarettes around their children. According to the Australian Institute of Health and Welfare (AIHW)[2] beer consumption was at its highest during this time, for people over fifteen years of age. As a country we were consuming between twelve to fourteen litres of pure alcohol per capita. My mum, however, wasn't a big drinker, only drinking on the odd occasion. Mum's drinking habits went against the statistics of the time and I completely took advantage of this opportunity to take a sip of her drink. I thought it tasted lovely, just like sweet cordial with an additional little zing. My lips and mouth felt tingly and almost a tad numb. After I had a taste, one just didn't seem enough. My parents and their friends always looked like they were having so much fun when they were drinking and I wanted to have fun too, so after that day I would occasionally have a sneaky sip from the fridge when no one was looking.

---

2. https://www.aihw.gov.au/reports/alcohol/alcohol-tobacco-other-drugs-australia/contents/drug-types/alcohol

Many students feel pressure in their first year of high school in some form or another. Mine was a particularly rocky one. I was eleven and just about to turn twelve when my parents divorced. I was a troublesome pre-teen. I wagged school, lied to my parents, brothers, sister, and schoolteachers. Although it didn't feel like it at the time it must have affected how I dealt with issues as I got older. I still kept my well-mannered demeanour but also had this side of me that needed to rebel. At the time though, I never really understood why. When I think about some teenagers these days, my behaviour was tame.

Overall, I felt as though I thought differently to my brothers and sister. I was a shy child with little self-confidence — I would constantly change my clothes, sometimes a few times in a day as I wanted people to think I looked pretty. Being an emotional child, I craved praise and affection. I also thought getting in trouble was the worst thing in the world, feeling like I had disappointed my parents terribly. This is when I started being terribly hard on myself and playing negative scenarios over and over in my head like a record. I would make a situation even worse in my head, which caused me to feel anxious.

I later learned there was a name for what was going on in my head — catastrophising. The Medical News Today Website in the UK[3] discusses catastrophising as cognitive distortion, meaning we will see an event as ultimately being disastrous.

Being fearful of losing things or people can get us into a catastrophising headspace, in particular if we hold them in high value telling ourselves things like - *'What if I ended up driving home drunk last night and then killed someone'* or *'if he hasn't called me by now, he's never going to*

---

3. https://www.medicalnewstoday.com/articles/320844#causes

call me, he's going to break up with me and I'll be alone forever.' Or, when people are unclear in their communication and give us a throw away comment like *'Please come and see me in my office when you are finished; I need to talk with you'* could then spiral into, *'What have I done? I'm going to get fired, I know it!'*

When I was around fifteen years old, I visited my cousins over the summer school holidays, in rural Victoria. We went to blue-light bush discos and would often have a few sips of Stones Green Ginger Wine before we made our way home. We enjoyed the feeling alcohol gave us so much that we drank more and more as we got older. At the time I felt like the alcohol made me feel relaxed and more confident. On the surface people thought I had all the confidence in the world, but underneath mostly I didn't really like myself and there were parts that I just loathed. Each summer, the more I drank, the more I would catastrophise and say to myself, *'Is mum going to know how much I've drunk?'* This was the beginning of my bigger binge drinking sessions. Of course, my mum didn't know I was drinking (or so I thought) when I went out with my cousins. Little did I know, my binge drinking sessions would later get heavier and messier as I got older.

 Mary's wisdom for living an alcohol-free life

Why **questions are not useful when trying to establish why you drink** – For me, *why* questions lead to fear and catastrophising, so I find it best to avoid these types of questions. You will however discover why you drink by asking yourself ***what***, ***when***, ***where*** and ***how*** questions.

For example:
Q: *What goes through my head and what do I feel in my body before I start drinking?*
A: *I get twitchy and start to feel as though I'm thirsty but I'm not thirsty at all. I see others drinking and I'm jealous. I then want a drink too.*
Q: *Where do I drink the most?*
A: *I used to drink when out in a group but now I drink on my own. This started because...*

Do you see how you will get clearer answers, rather than asking, 'Why? Why? Why?'

Communicate with people, if they are being unclear – I would often catastrophise when people were being unclear in their communication (read the example in the Chapter text above again if you are unsure). To avoid this, I talk to the person and ask them what they meant by what they said to you. By approaching the person and asking them specifically what they meant, avoids fear or a catastrophising spiral.

If you're still drinking, ask your friends to let you know when you have offended someone or started acting differently – This can cause you to be fearful or catastrophise, thinking you may have offended someone you love or care about. When I knew I wanted to quit, I asked my friends to let me know if I had offended or embarrassed them or someone else.

Breathe! – My mind is always drawn to catastrophising or fearful thoughts. It is about recognising when the thoughts arise that lead to this feeling, then start to take deep breaths to take your mind off those thoughts. Practising mindfulness is also very helpful.

Journal prompts...

Read the prompts below and in your journal, write as little or as much as you like. Not all of the questions may apply to your situation, so answer as many questions as you can.

Journaling about your thoughts and ideas helps you gain clarity and insight which may help you make better decisions when it comes to alcohol.

- **List four times when you were fearful** which led you to drink.
  - What were you fearful of and how were you feeling at the time, in both your body and mind? Be as descriptive as possible.
- **List two things (or people) you respect** which (or who) you lost and caused you to drink. From what you have listed, what made you drink on those two occasions? (Not just because you lost them/it – go deeper.
  - What about that person or thing did you hold in high value and what were the feelings you felt that made you want to drink?
- **Think of four positive statements** you can say to yourself when you think you are getting into a catastrophising (or fearful) headspace.
  - For example, 'I am a good person, whatever I have done can be resolved.' Another example is, 'Whatever this situation is telling me, it is nowhere near as bad as I think it is.'
- **If you were to stop drinking**, what would you fear losing? List three people or things.
- **Now think about if you were to continue to drink**, what are you now fearful of? List as many things you can think of.

Fear and Catastrophising

Living an Alcohol-free Life YOUR Way

Fear and Catastrophising

Chapter 2

Insecurities

'What I thought was 'letting my hair down', was simply covering up all of the horrible things I felt about myself.'
Mary Stuart

My really heavy big binge drinking sessions didn't start until the end of high school. When it came to the last day of high school, I knew this was a socially acceptable time I could drink heavily, with no barriers. Little did others around me know, I had been sneaking a few sips from the fridge for years. At the time I didn't quite understand what I was doing, but I later realised it was to cover my lack of self-confidence and insecurities.

Although I was seventeen at the time, this would be the first time I consumed a lot of alcohol in a short space of time. I felt ecstatic; I had looked forward to this day for a very long time, not only because I had just finished high school, but because I knew I could let my hair down, drink heavily, and people would not look at me weirdly for doing so. My good friend had just turned eighteen and a group of us tried to pressure her into buying our drinks for the evening. She didn't feel comfortable, so we asked my sister who was twenty at the time and she agreed. As I arrived at my friend's place around 3 p.m. in the afternoon, my sister had given me one bottle of Southern Comfort and one bottle of Midori. We both looked at the glossy brown and green liquid in the bottles with excitement. I said, *'Let's start drinking now!'* My friend's face changed from one of happiness to concern, *'Do you think that's a good idea? We have all night to drink.'* Disappointedly I replied, *'I suppose so.'* True to my now ingrained *sneaking style*, every time I went to the toilet, I grabbed the bottle of Midori out of the paper bottle-shop bag, sneaking a few sips before we even got ready to go out. My body was warming up from the inside out and I was starting to feel slightly flushed in the face. I was even starting to slur my words when my friend then said sternly, *'Have you started drinking? I can smell it on you!'* I nervously laughed, *'I've had a couple, it's no big deal, is it?'* almost asking for permission. She looked disappointed. I looked at her reassuringly, *'It's fine, we're going to have a ball tonight... aren't we?'* She smiled and excitedly said, *'C'mon, let's get ready!'*

I was a fun drunk – or *the paralytic nerd* as I was affectionately called back in the early 1990s. Extremely inappropriate nickname for these days, of course. Being the quiet, considerate, and polite student, as soon as the end of school celebrations started, I was loud, fun and the life of the party. I never felt as intelligent as people thought I was. Even though my Year 12 results were reasonable and nothing to be ashamed of, I lied to others in my year level and embellished my final score as I didn't want to feel or look stupid. I suppose I wanted to live up the studious *nerd* nickname with which people had labelled me. When I was in Year 12, if you were smart, people respected you. However, I often looked stupid anyway, as I would get drunk at parties. People often laughed at me, and I, in my drunken haze, would look around a room and could barely open my eyelids. It always felt like all eyes were on me. At the time, although I would have a small pang of embarrassment for a split second, I would then move on to not caring at all. I was enjoying drinking heavily for the first time in my life as it made me forget about my insecurities, if only for a while. What I thought was *letting my hair down*, was simply covering up all the horrible things I felt about myself. It's hard to pinpoint, but it may have just been the start of my love of drinking, because I was able to hide my insecurities.

Well, I thought I loved it anyway.

After my final year of high school there was many a night when we had parties or were invited to parties, and most of the time we would play drinking games until we were so drunk, I would slur my words, stumble and offend people. Every time I drank, I would never be just having a few drinks — once my foot was on the accelerator, I never hit the brake. I was once so drunk I tried to kiss a guy I really liked when out at a nightclub one night, but he turned me down, mainly because I was so drunk at the time — more to this story later in the book.

The only way I would end up home early was because I'd had so much, I had vomited, offended someone, or people had had enough of me and told me to go home. At this time, I was mainly drinking spirits like Southern Comfort and coke, or Midori and lemonade, then landing on vodka and raspberry as my chosen drink. Once the celebrations started at the end of school they never really stopped. The year after school we spent many a night at nightclubs getting completely *plastered* because I felt completely uncomfortable in my own skin. There were many parties where I was asked if I was drinking and I would always say yes. At that time, I don't think I ever went to a party alcohol-free.

As I often stayed over at my friend's place, there were many mornings I woke looking at the ceiling in her room, on the spare trundle bed, which was always uncomfortable. On one of those occasions, I lifted my head, then quickly let it hit the soft pillow underneath which left a spinning feeling which made me feel ill. I thought about the night before and immediately my mind started catastrophising. *'What happened last night? What did I say? Who did I annoy?'* The catastrophising which I experienced when I was younger was only exacerbated later in life. The voice just kept going around in my head the following morning. Every time without fail, as soon as my friend woke, I pretended I was fine, and I'd had a wonderful time the night before. I really could not remember a lot of it, and I would casually ask my friend what happened. She would always tell a story where I had done something stupid, kissed multiple people or got kicked out of venues for being too intoxicated. What an embarrassment; that I couldn't even remember what I had done the night before! Even though I made a mess of myself over and over again, I continued to do it for many years to come.

My mind would go into catastrophising mode and I would feel terrible about myself and the others who I hurt or embarrassed. I felt like I wasn't good enough, both physically and mentally. At times couldn't keep up with conversations which made me feel stupid, I felt fat and frumpy and had done for most of my life. It didn't help when people called you fat, or the time someone you respected called you jellybum, or the guy at school who you liked didn't like you back. I would often say to myself, *'Why doesn't he like me, IS my bum fat?'* Then I convinced myself that others were right. The culmination of all of those things over time just made me feel worthless. Although I thought I drank to dull those thoughts for a while, drinking just made those thoughts in my head worse.

 Mary's wisdom for living an alcohol-free life

Feeling like you don't know as much as others when talking in a group of people is normal. Remember, there is always another person feeling the same way! I found that increasing my general knowledge and being interested in what is going on in the world will make that uncomfortable feeling disappear when talking in a group of people. This is not about impressing others; it's about making you feel better about yourself. Also, I found it is okay just to listen and admit you are unsure of a topic of conversation. You don't have to know everything, and you don't have to feel bad about that. People also love a good listener. Remember, it can be an opportunity for you to learn something!

Insecurities causing an increase in alcohol consumption. I would drink alcohol due to lack of self-confidence, the desire to please others, and rebellion. Being uncomfortable in your own skin is obviously a trigger to drinking (well it was for me). Working on your insecurities will help you to feel better about yourself, which will then help you not to drink as much.

Being the life of the party (when drunk) is not all it's cracked up to be. Getting completely drunk at parties can get you labelled a laughingstock after a while. You can also wake up the next morning finding you can't remember what happened which can send you into a catastrophising spiral, which can in turn bruise your ego. Consistently acting like this will more than likely increase your insecurities.

> **Worrying that others are talking about you.** There is no point spending your time thinking about what other people think of you. Also, they may not be talking about you at all. Worrying about this constantly can play havoc with your insecurities.

 Journal prompts...

Just like Chapter 1, read the prompts below and in your journal, write as little or as much as you like. Not all of the questions may apply to your situation, so answer as many questions as you can.

Remember journaling about your thoughts and ideas helps you gain clarity and insight, which may help you make better decisions when it comes to alcohol.

- **What was your self-confidence like as a child/teenager?** I'm not talking about whether you looked like (or pretended) you were confident, how did you actually feel?
- **Did you drink as a young person?**
  – If so, did you feel like you couldn't take your foot off the accelerator?
  – What were you feeling to make you do this? Be as descriptive as possible.
- **If you still have the above feelings now**, list three positive statements you can say to yourself when you feel this way.
  OR
  If you had positive feelings when you were a child, do you still feel this way or has something changed? If changed, list three things that have changed.
- **Describe two situations** where your insecurities took over. What did you physically feel? For example, *did your palms get sweaty, face go red, you felt warm all over, twitchy, etc.*

- **Now describe the complete opposite** to the situations you described above. For example, *I was happy and smiling and immediately walked up to someone I didn't know and introduced myself.*
  - Try attempting something that makes you feel uncomfortable, such as introducing yourself to people you don't know very well. Record this in your journal about how it went. How did you feel? Be as descriptive as possible.

** If you are still drinking, remember to write how you are feeling each day, when you are triggered or craving a drink, hungover or any other times you think about alcohol. Reading your journal regularly will help to change the way you think about alcohol. You can also do this if you have quit drinking, but you can write about situations where you were drunk and how you were feeling at that time.

Insecurities

Chapter 3
Drinking 'Friends'

'I was no stranger to binge drinking at this stage and it was my pattern to 'go hard or go home'. I could never just have a few drinks when out.'
Mary Stuart

I was nineteen and I had been working in hospitality for a while and it was the first time I was drinking heavily over consecutive nights. I made friends with a co-worker who was an older lady in her forties. She was an interesting character and I wanted to get to know her better. She lived in a small, bohemian-style place, not far from work and appeared to have a life of freedom. Drinking glasses of wine every night, playing music until late, having clever, intelligent conversations with friends. Her life from the outside looked perfect to me. This is what I wanted for my life; that freedom but also to be very *put together* rather than feeling like the laughingstock every time I drank.

I thought I was getting to know her more but all I was really doing was being pressured into doing what she wanted, which would always involve drinking. I never felt like I was being myself. I was no stranger to binge drinking at this stage and it was my pattern to *go hard or go home*. I could never just have a few drinks because I was always anxious around other people when out. The alcohol calmed me down, so it meant I kept drinking as soon as I started. My work *friend* knew this about me and would encourage me to drink more, even when I didn't want to. She was quite manipulative and was always encouraging one of the guys we worked with to come out with us so we could drink more. She knew I liked him. *'C'mon Mary, you don't have to go home...your boyfriend will wait up for you...come out with us!'* she would plead. Even when I'd had a lot to drink after she always encouraged me to drink more and more. At the time my instincts were telling me it didn't seem right, but I wanted her to like me.

When I was out, there were times I wouldn't be following the conversation, my mind felt like I was in a daze, my eyes blurry and I kept pretending to fit in. At the time I was quite naïve, and I did not feel as intelligent as the others in the group. As a young person, I hadn't really taken in a lot of what was going on in the world. I wasn't up with local politics or any politics, for that matter. I didn't feel like it was important, but it always seemed like people knew more than I did. This was another reason why I drank, *'Make people laugh Mary...do your circus tricks,'* is what would go on in my head. I was definitely the jester of any group, wherever I was. Whenever others would start talking about a topic I knew nothing about, I would say to myself, *'Show people how funny you are.'* I wanted to fit in and feel wanted. I had a quick wit and this, at the time, was one of only a few things I liked about myself, so I used it to my advantage.

To this day, I don't know if I was ever truly friends with this woman I worked with and I'm not sure what she was getting out of pressuring me to get so drunk, that I was acting in a way I wouldn't normally. We always ended up back at her place, along with the guy I liked. During one drinking stint (which was over the course of three nights) I ended up kissing him which subsequently ended my relationship with my boyfriend at the time. This guy was very charismatic – he loved women and women loved him. When I met him, he had a girlfriend which didn't last long. Before I knew it, I was in a casual, secret relationship and no one knew but my older work friend. He, on the other hand, was only in it for the triumph as I was significantly younger than him. As soon as I had slept with him, he pretended I didn't exist. Before I knew it, people were talking about me at work. One night I caught one of the sous chefs in the kitchen late at night laughing at how oblivious I was, getting used by this man. I was so embarrassed and humiliated, I grabbed my oversized jacket and scarf and ran out of the restaurant into the dark, cold night and briskly walked all the way down the street. My embarrassment soon turned into anger and hatred for everyone I worked with. About fifteen minutes later the chef drove past and she asked me to get in the car so we could go for a drink. I said no thanks and kept walking. I could see on her face; she knew I had heard her talking about me in the kitchen. I resigned from that job only a few days later. I knew the embarrassment and humiliation was from being young, stupid and being pressured into drinking more than I could handle at the time. Unfortunately, I didn't really learn from this experience and the pattern would continue for many years to come.

When I was twenty years old, I was working in hospitality at a restaurant in Melbourne – it was a lovely, luxe, wooden panelled restaurant with heavy, solid rosewood tables and large heavy wicker chairs. I became friends with an American waitress who was friendly and easy to talk to, the only problem was, she was a big drinker. It had come to the end of the year and our boss, who was normally pretty tight with his money, said we could drink whatever we wanted from the bar on our last shift before the Christmas break. The American waitress and I got so drunk, we then decided to go out afterwards to a dingy pub in a shady Melbourne suburb. During the night I was paranoid she was making fun of me with her boyfriend. My vision blurred, I stumbled out of the pub and ended up walking down a back street. As I was walking, my stomach was doing somersaults and I felt like my legs would give way at any moment. I ended up down the dark street, my breathing laboured and almost felt like my heartbeat was in my mouth. I felt sick, so I fell to the ground and sat in the gutter for a while. When not drinking, I would never just fall into a gutter, but this is how drunk I was. I knew I was going to be sick; the wave came over me and I felt a surge through my body and before I knew it, I saw vomit all over the road and in the gutter.

All of a sudden, I saw a bright light coming closer and closer toward me, then I saw two. It was a car pulling over near me. A man came running from the driver's side and said with what seemed to be an Indian accent, *'Would you like to get in the car?'* As I struggled to raise my head and to try and pull myself up, I saw the car was yellow and realised it was a cab. I slurred and mumbled, *'I'm OK, I'm really sick so it probably wouldn't be a good idea.'* Unfortunately, I spent most of the ride with my head out the window, my stomach convulsing and vomiting with no control. The vomit splattered against the cab, as though I was on the Gravitron at Luna Park. The cab driver did not care, he seemed to have more compassion for me and wanted to get me home. It was very unusual, as a cab driver would normally expect you to clean up the mess, but it was almost like he knew I had a bad night and just needed to get home in one piece. I was very thankful for that cab driver as I may have been sitting in that gutter in that dodgy part of town for the rest of the evening. I drank and drank to excess and did not think much as I was in my twenties and thought I was invincible.

Wanting people to like us and not gossip about us is a common reason to abuse alcohol. Feeling like people won't like us is a common reason for us to turn to alcohol and feel like it is going to make everything feel better. However, we soon realise it doesn't, when we wake up with a hangover or just feeling like rubbish in general. Gossiping is a negative activity associated with alcohol use, due to people being *loose lipped*, and in my experience can lead to catastrophising which can lead to alcohol becoming an addiction, where your body starts to crave it.

 Mary's wisdom for living an alcohol-free life

Determine whether people are your real friends – I found it helpful to ask your work *friend* out for a coffee or an activity that doesn't involve drinking. This is helpful to see if you are considered more than just a *drinking buddy*.

What other people think of you is none of your business – As I touched on in Chapter 2, this is a hard one and it took me many years to realise that what other people think of you, is none of your business. Of course, I'm not referring to true friends that will be there for you no matter what. I'm talking about the type of person who says they are your friend but feels the need to gossip about you behind your back.

Drinking cultures will always exist as long as alcohol is around – Having strategies for how you can deal with this culture in a positive way is very helpful in assisting you to move forward, alcohol-free.

> **When you are drinking to excess** – It can cause you to engage in risky behaviour. Having *friends* that don't look out for you when drunk is also risky. Ensure when you go out you have a good friend (with whom you have previously agreed) who will look after you to ensure you don't make bad decisions.

 Journal prompts...

- **Think about a time** when you were around people drinking and you were involved in some questionable behaviour and your gut was telling you *this is wrong*, but you did it anyway. Write down as many of those experiences as you can. For example, *leaving a bar with a stranger and you end up at a hotel with a room full of people you don't know.*
- **Choose two of those experiences and list** one positive thing (each) you would do differently. Using the example above, *politely decline the invitation to go back with the stranger and ensure you are around friends when you tell them, in case things get nasty.*
- **List four positive statements** you can say to yourself to avoid getting drawn in by negative influences.
  – For example, *'I'm happy to be driving home from this party, alcohol-free.' 'I feel healthy and happy being alcohol-free.'*
- **Do you find you make the same types of** *friends* **when drinking?**
  – What do those friends look like? List three characteristics.
  – What defines those friendships? List three things.
- **Make a list of all of the toxic people** in your life.
  – List one thing for each person on your list that makes them toxic. For example, *"They try to pressure me to drink, even when they know I don't want to."*
  – What boundaries can you put in place to deal with those people? For example, *whether you can avoid this person (because they may be a*

friend or family member) just say no to those drinks and stand by your conviction OR *decide you don't want this person in your life.*

Living an Alcohol-free Life YOUR Way

Drinking 'Friends'

Chapter 4

Being someone you are not

'Being single wasn't easy for me and at the time there was no other way to describe it; I was a complete mess. Going from one guy to the next, trying to find my perfect man.'

Mary Stuart

I married my first husband when I was twenty-two. He would binge drink most weeks – Thursday, Friday, Saturday and Sunday, so it was easy for me to binge drink through most of my first marriage, drinking heavily at parties, weddings and other events. I spent most of this relationship doing whatever he wanted to do. We bought a house in a suburb where he wanted to live, and I passively agreed. I didn't want to disappoint him as it was, after all, near the cricket and football club, which was going to be much easier for him to socialise with his family, friends and his social circle. I went to many of my friends' weddings or events on my own because he had to play cricket or football. I very rarely voiced my concerns, which wasn't healthy. After many years this made me miserable and I realised I should have never married him in the first place.

I remember attending a wedding with him, where I felt quite uncomfortable and insecure, politely smiling at people. I did not know anyone as the groom was a work friend of my husband. It was unusual to me as half of the room was served Italian food and the other half Albanian food, and the guests on the Albanian tables were not served alcohol. Of course, we were on a table which was exactly halfway between the two sides of the room. Although we were served alcohol there was a moment where I was nervously sitting in my seat anxiously thinking, 'Are we going to be drinking or not? This is crazy; where is the alcohol? I don't know any of these people, how am I going to cope?' I looked across to the Italian side of the room, then to the Albanian side nervously waiting whether I would be stuck in an anxiety bubble for the rest of the evening. Once again, I would catastrophise the situation, it just became a part of my life. As the alcohol arrived, I would drink and drink quickly, so I had enough courage to talk to people I had only just met. Of course, the situation was nowhere near as bad as I first thought. Even though I understood this, little did I know I would play stories such as this over and over in my head in the years to come.

Toward the later part of my marriage, when I knew it was doomed, I would wait until my husband was in bed and sneak into the pantry to get a nightcap. My eyes would dart to the kitchen doorway and listen to see if I heard rustling from the bedroom. When I confirmed the coast was clear, I would then turn the light on, grab the Kahlua bottle from the top shelf, then a large coffee cup from the cupboard, pour some chocolate-brown Kahlua into the bottom quarter of the cup then quickly place the bottle back onto the top shelf. My eyes would once again dart toward the door and listen for any movement, I would then add some milk to the bottom of the cup along with some powdered chocolate. I placed the cup next to the kettle, patiently waiting for it to boil and monitored it like an army soldier, in case he woke and saw what I was doing. I suppose this is where my binge drinking turned into daily drinking. Deep down, I knew that it was wrong, but I still did it and continued to binge drink and also had the nightly *nightcap*.

We were married for almost eight years and we divorced when I was thirty.

Around seven months after my marriage ended, I started dating a close friend of mine from work. Our whole relationship was based around drinking and occasionally taking drugs. We constantly enabled each other and when either of us were on our way home from work we would get more wine. My life at that stage just became about drinking, drinking and more drinking. Yes, I was socialising at this stage, but later in that relationship my drinking just got worse and nightly drinking at home, either alone or with him, just became the norm. He did not like a lot of my good friends and because of this, I dropped them one by one. I thought at the time this made me happy, but I was just moulding myself into what he wanted me to be. I was drinking at 12 p.m. on a Saturday and Sunday where we would often jokingly say, *'It's 5 p.m. somewhere in the world!'* He was a smoker, so of course (when I was drinking) I smoked cigarettes, heavily. Although the relationship ended five years later, I continued to drink daily. I was thirty-five.

After eight months of being in and out of short-term relationships, I then ended up single. Being single wasn't easy for me and at the time there was no other way to describe it; I was a complete mess. Going from one guy to the next, trying to find my perfect man. But in the meantime, I was just trying to fit into other people's lives rather than being with people who truly liked me for me. My insecurities were mostly my downfall in relationships. Mostly thinking I wasn't good enough. This totally put guys off.

Since my first marriage ended, my drinking got so bad that it truly was like being on a really bad ride; I knew I was going to vomit, but the ride master would not let me off. Then, when I did vomit, it splattered all over everyone else in the back carriages. When I did finally get off the ride, the ride master told me to apologise to the people in the back and to clean up, but I would just shrug and walk away. This is how my life was for a while – feeling very little for others around me and in particular for myself.

I lost many good friends during this time as I felt, at the time, they were not there for me. I felt sorry for myself and had a victim mentality and pushed all my good friends away, one by one. Some friends I had known for many years and lost and others I have rebuilt over time. The problem was, I allowed my partner's (and my drinking) to dictate who I saw and who I was friends with. Basically, I was a doormat and was doing things to please others, even though that person may not have been the most compatible person for me. Some would say I was a chameleon and would change myself according to the partner I was with at the time. Little did I know I would end up with the person who was right for me all along.

Mary's wisdom for living an alcohol-free life

Doing things to please others – Pleasing others in a relationship and trying to morph yourself into their life almost always ends in disaster. It is great to be giving and loving to your partner and friends, but not at the expense of your self-esteem. Always think, *'Am I doing this because I want to, or am I doing it because the person I'm with wants to?'*

Be yourself – Remember you have many good qualities, so focus on those when people are trying to take advantage of you.

Learn to say no to others – People may – intentionally or unintentionally – try and coerce you into doing what they want. Remember it's okay to compromise but not at the expense of your own values and beliefs.

Remember to always be honest with yourself! If it doesn't feel right, then ask yourself *why*. Listen to your intuition; it's there for a reason.

 Journal prompts...

- **Name four negative things** you do to please other people. For example, *brushing off your friends to do what your partner wants* OR *You stop doing what you love doing (something healthy) just because your partner hates it.*
- **Now choose three things** from the list and write what you would say to those people when you want to say no. Preferably choose items that relate to or have an impact on your drinking.
- **Name four good qualities** you have identified about yourself. If you cannot think of any yourself, then ask a friend or family member. For example, *bubbly personality, highly intelligent, emotionally intelligent*

- **When have you engaged in** what you consider risky behaviour? Explain what happened using one example. Be specific as possible. For example, *a one-night stand, where were you? What were you doing to get into that situation?*
- **If you were being honest with yourself** what would you be doing instead of pleasing others. **List four alternative activities.** For example, *Walking the dog, reading your favourite book, attending art classes.*

Being someone you are not

Living an Alcohol-free Life YOUR Way

Being someone you are not

Chapter 5

Telling others

'I felt numb and felt like my life was just not worth continuing. I hadn't reached the point where I was suicidal, but I felt lonely and I was looking to others (and alcohol) to make me feel better.'

Mary Stuart

The first time I decided to stop drinking, I was in a pretty low place and I really thought I had hit what people call rock bottom. That day I decided to quit, one of my old friends had just passed away from a long battle with cancer. *'Thirty-seven years of age, he was so young,'* I thought. *'What am I doing with my life?'* I remember driving in the car on a cold and wet evening. I called my best friend and told her; *'I've really decided this time... I want to quit drinking.'* She went quiet and that's when I knew she was crying. *'I'm so proud of you honey, I know you can do this,'* she said. I felt numb; like my life was just not worth continuing. I hadn't reached the point where I was suicidal, but I felt lonely and I was looking to others (and alcohol) to make me feel better.

I attended the funeral of my high school friend with my mum. We both walked into the church where we found we were the first few people to arrive. We sat in a pew halfway down on the right-hand side of the church. My brother and sister-in-law arrived, and after we kissed and hugged, they settled into the pew in front of us. I stared to the front of the church and sobbed, thinking about my friend, remembering his cheekiness and what an absolute tragedy it was. As I bawled, my mum held my hand and said, *'It's going to be OK.'* She handed me a crumpled tissue she pulled from her bag, placed it near my hand and said, *'Here, take this.'* As I wiped my eyes and runny nose, I turned and noticed the church was full and there were more people out in the foyer. There was now standing room only. I'm guessing people just couldn't believe that someone so young could die. It was lovely that so many people came to pay their respects to such a wonderful person. The music started playing and the family walked in together – two people walked either side of his wife as she cried uncontrollably. The poor woman was inconsolable and could barely walk on her own. Her grief only compounded the feelings of others around her, including myself. It was difficult not to experience some of the pain that she was feeling.

As we walked out of the church, there were so many people that I turned to mum and said, *'We'll pay our respects at the wake, there's way too many people here.'* She nodded. I told her to wait undercover as it was now raining heavily. I put my coat over my head and ran across the street to my car. I then drove my car over to mum and collected her. She jumped in the passenger seat and sighed, *'Wow, it's pouring out there!'* I replied, *'It sure is mama.'*

As I was driving away from the church with the wipers on high speed, the rain swooshing across the windscreen, I quietly said, *'I have something to tell you, mum.'* Mum always panicked every time I said this, and she anxiously asked, *'What is it?'*

'I have a problem with alcohol, mum.' I felt ashamed. She started to cry and said, *'Oh Mary, what do you mean?'* I replied, *'I've had a problem for a long time now mum. I just didn't want you to know, I knew you would worry.'* I began to cry and kept saying, *'I'm sorry mama, I'm so sorry.'* She then said, *'Oh Mary, don't be sorry and you know you can always come to me and tell me anything. Are you getting help?'* I paused, then said, *'I think I need to see a counsellor; it's out of control.'* I wanted to protect my mum by not telling her all the details. I wanted her to continue to have this view about me, that sweet innocent *Mary Poppins,* a nickname she used to call me as a kid. As my mum did not drink, I didn't want her to have this idea I was getting so drunk where I was behaving erratically – even though this was, in fact, true. My mum always reassured me in situations such as this. She may not have felt like she knew what to say, but she always managed to make me feel comforted. This was only the beginning of my discussions with my mum.

Justifying why we shouldn't tell someone else about our drinking is common, in particular for those who mean so much to us. It's the same old story, that we want to show this façade to others to believe we have everything under control. I'm not suggesting this is easy or that the very first time you decide to raise this you will have the perfect conversation. We just need to be honest with ourselves about how much we drink and letting others know about this is a great start!

Mary's wisdom for living an alcohol-free life

How can you tell someone that you have a problem with drinking?

Be honest – For me this was one of the main reasons why I have remained living an alcohol-free life. For you it will be a freeing experience and one you will remember forever. It's worth it; give it a go!

Open your heart and tell them exactly how you are feeling – I told my mum exactly how I was feeling. Whoever you tell, they will either understand or not; you can't control this. It will also make you feel better by getting everything off your chest. If the person you tell chooses to walk away, remember this is not your issue, it's theirs! Accept they have a difference of opinion. Don't let this stop you from achieving your goal of living an alcohol-free life!

Tell them how much you are drinking – Going back to the first point. Be very honest about your drinking, how much and how often. This will give them an idea of how they can support you through the first stages of living an alcohol-free life.

Let them know how they can support you through this time – Think about how your friends and family can support you. Although this never worked for me, you may want to cut back in the beginning and ask your friends to help monitor your drinking. Another strategy is to give your friends your bank card before you go out, this way, you are accountable for how much you drink.

Journal prompts...

- **Who is someone in your life** you feel you should share your relationship with alcohol with? If there is more than one person, list them and explain why you would want them to know. For example, *it could be your wife/ husband/partner and maybe you want them to know how you feel when you crave a drink.*
  - What would you tell them? Be descriptive. If it helps, write down and practice what you would say.
- **What support do you need** from a loved one? For example, *it could be as simple as a hug when you need it.*
- **If you don't feel comfortable** sharing your relationship with alcohol with those closest to you, is there someone else you know who won't judge you but will listen to you? Once again, write what you would say to them, as it may be different to what you would say to a loved one.
- **Write down four possible defensive comments** you may receive from your loved one or person you trust. For example *'Why are you not drinking? You've changed!'* Now write four assertive, positive responses to those comments. For example, *'I'm not drinking because I'm better company without it.'*
- **What are you fearful of** when you think about telling someone about your drinking? List everything that comes to mind. For example, *'They will judge me'* OR *'They will think I'm a drunk and look down on me.'*

Living an Alcohol-free Life YOUR Way

Telling others

Chapter 6

Going out, without a plan

'I felt like people were judging me even though I was in a group engaging in conversation. I can't describe it any other way, I just felt completely and utterly alone and awkward.'

Mary Stuart

It had been two weeks of going cold turkey and a friend called me to attend a Halloween party in Melbourne's North. Initially I said, somewhat ashamedly, *'No I don't think it's a good idea, I have only just stopped drinking.' 'Oh c'mon...YOU, not drinking?!'* she laughed. *'You'll be fine; c'mon it will be fun!'* she insisted. It was a friend who I didn't consider a good friend but who was fun to go out with, usually when I was drinking. What was going through my head was; *'Do you trust yourself to go? Can you be there and not drink..?'* My friend kept saying it would be fun and we'd be catching up with old friends. She also said if I did drink, it wouldn't be the worst thing in the world. I agreed to go and told her I would drive and pick her up at 7 p.m. I had no idea how I was going to do this; I simply had no plan.

I drank Diet Coke like it was alcohol; I must have had eight cans during the evening and smoked almost three quarters of a packet of cigarettes. I wasn't a regular smoker; I would, however, smoke heavily when out at parties. During the day I could take it or leave it. To be honest, as people started to get drunker, the noise got louder, and I just wanted to leave. They looked like they were having so much fun and at the time I felt like the awkward person drinking Diet Coke and sitting outside smoking cigarettes. I felt like people were judging me even though I was in a group, engaging in conversation. My insecurities during situations like this were playing havoc and the catastrophising would begin. Also, my brain would try to talk me out of living an alcohol-free life. *'Why am I sitting here looking like an idiot, when I could be drinking and having fun like the rest of them?'* I can't describe it any other way, I just felt completely and utterly awkward and alone.

A few nights later the same *friend* asked me to a pub in South Melbourne. I said I would be there as I thought the previous party could have just been a one-off for me, surely this had to be better. I arrived and people were laughing, sitting outside around trestle tables on a beautiful, Australian, balmy summer's night. All I felt like was a nice cold glass of Sauvignon Blanc. My skin was crawling, but I managed to plaster a fake smile on my face, grabbed a glass of water and lit a cigarette. I took a seat on the bench while others were standing around me, laughing and drinking their alcoholic drinks. After a few hours we went inside, and this is when things got progressively worse. I felt like I was walking through water and everything seemed to get dark and dingy. All of a sudden, people were grabbing me on the backside and guys were talking to me, up really close with their foul-smelling breath and attempting to pull me in closer. Once they knew I wasn't drinking they would move on to the next girl that maybe was drunk, of whom they could take advantage. As I looked around the room, I felt myself getting angrier and angrier.

There was an older guy who was part of the group but who I had only just met, and he was also a non-drinker but was making me feel uncomfortable as he was talking to me even though I wasn't engaging all that much. As I kept moving away from him, he kept moving closer and saying things like, *'Us non-drinkers have to stick together, don't we?'* He seemed sleazy, occasionally touching me on my hand or arm when he spoke with me and then moving closer, pretending as though it was because the music was loud. Me, politely smiling and not really listening to what he was saying, as my mind wandered, and my eyes darted around the room. Eventually, I just looked at him and turned to my *friend* who had invited me and said, *'I have to go, your friend is being really sleazy, and I don't like it.'* She dropped her bottom lip and gave me a patronising look which seemed to be an *'I feel sorry for you'* face and hugged me. I quickly snuck out the side door so that guy wouldn't notice and ran to my car, frantically looking behind me two or three times in quick succession, in case he came out looking for me. My car was only a few doors down from the pub, so once I arrived, opened the door and sighed heavily as I sat in the driver's seat. As I scanned the street to see if there were any suspicious-looking people around, I locked the doors and cried. I felt left out, alone and maybe this wasn't going to work. I then started thinking, *'Maybe I was wrong, this alcohol-free life is not all it's cracked up to be, I have no idea how long I can do this for.'*

Mary's wisdom for living an alcohol-free life

Try going out without drinking – this is a good way to see how much alcohol has a hold on you. If you find it difficult then leave and go home. It can't hurt to give it a go! This can also determine whether you are truly ready to live an alcohol-free life.

Be honest if people ask why you are not drinking – As stated in Chapter 5 this is one of the main reasons why I have remained living an alcohol-free life; being honest. Some will call you a buzz-kill but hopefully answering the questions in the previous chapters will increase your self-confidence enough to not let it bother you.

Try to talk with people who are sober or not that drunk – I found the key to enjoying a party is to gravitate to people who either don't drink or who are drinking very little. This way you can have a decent conversation without getting those pangs of feeling left out.

Have a plan of how you will approach an event – Decide how long you are going to stay for and at what point you will leave. Decide what you will drink for the evening. Also decide at what point will you not put up with bad behaviour and also decide if this is a point when you will leave.

 Journal prompts...

Reminder! Remember your journal is not there to write and leave; it's there to write and read! Make sure you read over what you have written on a regular basis as this will build your alcohol-free muscle.

- **When you are going to a party/event, what is your plan?**
  Here are some questions you may want to ask yourself when developing a plan:
  – How are you getting there? Who are you going with?
  – What are you going to drink?
  – Who is going to be there?
  – If they are people you don't know well (or like) what strategies will you put in place to cope with being around them?
  – What time will you leave when things are starting to get out of control? *i.e. when you start to feel uncomfortable.*
- **List five reasons that cause you to drink when out**, for example, *fidgeting when nervous or sitting on your own as you are uncomfortable around others.*
  – **Now, using the five reasons above, add five positive alternate things you can do.** For example, *say hello to one person you don't know.*
- **Name two thoughts that go through your mind** when you see others drunk when you are out. For example, *'I can't believe they are drinking without me.'* OR *'They look like they are having so much fun!'*
  – **Now name two affirmations you can say to yourself** when you see others drunk when you are out. For example, *'If I don't drink I won't have a hangover tomorrow and I'll wake up refreshed!'* OR *'Alcohol is a poison and ruins my relationships.'*
- **Do you have a story you repeat over and over** when out with people to excuse your drinking or behaviour?
  – If so, what is the story? What can you do to change the story? OR could you stop telling the story?
- **How will you say no** to a drink when offered one at a party? Name two things you could say.

Living an Alcohol-free Life YOUR Way

Going out, without a plan

Chapter 7
Antidepressants and counselling

'During the session I listened intently, hanging off her every word and was very open about how I felt and the things I had experienced while I was drinking.'
Mary Stuart

There was a period when I experienced depression, which may have been due to my situation, or my excessive alcohol use. Either way, I was a mess, and I couldn't sleep, I never wanted to go to work and quite simply never wanted to get out of bed. At the time, I needed to see a doctor as I wasn't good at all. My family doctor prescribed Endep (an antidepressant) and all it made me feel was nothing. I didn't feel happy and I didn't feel sad, I just felt *nothing*. It regulated my sleep which was a positive, however being an emotional person and not really having any feelings was not doing much for me. I remember having a conversation with my estranged sister over the phone and she said I sounded cold. After she called me an alcoholic and that I didn't understand what she was going through, knowing she had issues of her own, I did not want to then disclose that I was depressed. Growing up I had a great relationship with my sister, but as we got older all it turned into angry and emotional phone conversations. The story related to how we got to that point is a long one, a story for another time. Being called an alcoholic was not something I enjoyed as I linked it to when I was younger, hearing it used as a name for a person who didn't have their life together.

I had been seeing an addiction counsellor through a community organisation where I had six on-on-one sessions. During my first session I was keen to discover why I drank and had high hopes these sessions were going to help me understand why I drank and give me strategies I could put in place for times when I felt like I needed to drink. I remember waiting in the reception area being so proud of myself for getting there, but at the same time thinking, *'What are you doing here? You are not this person, a problem with alcohol? NO! Maybe I should leave before the counsellor comes out, no one would know any better.'* That was just my brain playing tricks with me. I aimlessly looked through trashy magazines that were two to three years old pretending to like them so no one would pay attention to me and occasionally let my eyes scan the room, just in case I saw someone I knew.

I remember seeing the counsellor for the first time. She had a long flowing skirt, a large, oversized shirt, and long dreadlocks. *'Mary?'* I stood up and she looked at me with a warm smile. She introduced herself and said, *'Come with me.'* I walked into a small, box-like room where they had attempted to make it welcoming, with a plant in the corner, two-comfortable looking chairs and a small round table separating them. She asked, *'So, Mary, what has prompted you to be here?'* 'Well, I feel

Antidepressants and counselling

like I have an issue with alcohol,' I replied, as I ashamedly put my head down. Almost like I was asking for her opinion as to whether I did or not. *'Right, would you like to talk about that further? Has an event or incident prompted you to book an appointment with me?'.* 'Yes.' I paused and then continued, *'My friend from high school died after a long battle with cancer. His death just made me think it is time to take a good look at my drinking habits and to attempt to get a hold of it.'*

She then went on to ask about my drinking habits and I spoke about my daily drinking and how I felt as though I had been in a cycle for years. During the session I listened intently, hanging off her every word and was very open about how I felt and the things I had experienced while I was drinking. She gave me homework and I went home and completed a worksheet about what I did when drunk and how I felt. I then went back for the remaining five sessions, but I felt they did not pack the same punch as the first. For the remaining sessions, I sat there thinking about anything other than what she was discussing, analysing her clothes and wondering about what she did when she went home. *'Did she drink?'* I thought. Once she forgot to address the homework she gave me, then I switched off. I thought, *'If she isn't going to follow through, then why should I?'* Once again, my mind would play tricks so I would be drawn back into drinking.

I started drinking again only a few days after my last counselling session and decided antidepressants and counselling were not for me. There had to be another way for me to feel like my old self without resorting to drinking as much as I was. I later learned there was indeed another way, without having to take prescription drugs or pour my heart out to a complete stranger.

Antidepressants and counselling are commonly used when someone has been using alcohol for some time as a way to alleviate their depression. Whether the depression is exacerbated by the alcohol consumption or you have already been living with depression, antidepressants and counselling can be a good way to assist you in getting better. This is something you need to weigh up, whether either are right for you.

Please note – if you are physically dependent on alcohol, where you feel like you need alcohol to function every day, making an appointment with a health professional or psychologist is the best course of action.

> **Mary's wisdom for living an alcohol-free life**
>
> How can you tell if you need counselling/Alcoholics Anonymous (AA), detoxification/rehabilitation or other services/products?
>
> **Be honest with yourself about where your drinking is at** – if you have reached a point where you feel like it's out of your control, then maybe counselling, detox/rehab, withdrawal drugs or AA is something that will suit you. Making an appointment to see your family doctor might be the best course of action to start.
>
> **Determine if the service aligns with your values** – Does the service you are considering align with your personal values? If not, it may not be the right approach for you.
>
> **Determine if you are comfortable talking in groups or individual sessions** – For me, I wasn't comfortable talking in groups and wasn't comfortable sharing with other people I did not know. One-on-one

Antidepressants and counselling

counselling sessions might be something you might want to consider if you don't feel comfortable talking to a loved one.

Always go in with a plan – I found when I was seeing a counsellor that going in with a clear idea of what you want to discuss can assist in getting the most out of the sessions.

 Journal prompts...

- **Look at the positives and negatives** of utilising an alcohol support service and/or taking antidepressants. Draw a line down the centre of a page in your journal. Write positives on one side and negatives on the other. Then write what the positives would be of going to counselling/AA or any other external support service, then repeat but now write the negatives. Do the same for whether or not antidepressants are right for you (including what your health professional advises).
- **Decide what makes you feel more comfortable.** Do you prefer talking to a stranger or someone you are close to? (If it is someone you are close to, refer back to the Journal Prompts in Chapter 5.)
- **Decide if you will go it alone.** What strategies will you put in place? Will you enlist others for support?
- **Decide what you will say.** I'm not saying to write out everything you will say to a counsellor or in an AA meeting, but it is good to be prepared about the points you want to raise. This will give you a good start and it will encourage you to talk more.
- **What are you hoping to get out of discussions with the service you engage with?** Decide on an outcome from the sessions. Go ahead and ask yourself the following questions:
    – Do you want to quit altogether, or merely cut down?
    – What kind of support are you after? For example, *do you just want to get*

things off your chest, OR *do you want to get to the bottom of why you drink?*
- What if you discover something you didn't know about yourself? Would you want to explore this further?

Antidepressants and counselling

Living an Alcohol-free Life YOUR Way

Antidepressants and counselling

Chapter 8

Dating and Relationships

'Alcohol blinded me so I could not see what was in front of me, in that it was contributing to my failing relationships.'

Mary Stuart

It was my thirty-sixth birthday and I wanted to get drunk as I had been so good with going to counselling. My housemate and I threw a party and lots of friends arrived, including many people I had not seen for quite some time. As usual, I started drinking very early and very quickly. By about 9.30 p.m. I was chatting to people when all of a sudden, in slow motion, I saw my red wine fly across the pastel green carpet. I tried to stop it, but my reaction was too slow and I fell straight into it, leaving a massive red wine stain on the carpet and all down the side of my dress. Everyone around me was laughing and two friends grabbed me on either side and took me downstairs to my bathroom. One grabbed me another dress from my bedroom and the other came into the bathroom while I was sitting on the edge of the bathtub and said, *'Mary, Mary, what are* you doing?' I slurred, *'I don't need a lecture, thanks for the help, but you can go now!'* I pulled myself up (with the assistance of the towel rail) and stumbled out of the bathroom and went straight back upstairs, my breathing laboured. I walked out the front door, missed the step and proceeded to smack my chin on the brick retainer wall. My housemate was behind me, laughing, *'Are you okay?'* And as he grabbed my arm to help me up, he laughed. I pulled my arm away from his, as I hated people laughing at me when I was drunk. I slurred, *'I'm fine, leave me alone.'* Even though I was really drunk I always knew when people were being sarcastic or making fun of me. I'm surprised I didn't break my jaw and end up in hospital. Of course, I didn't feel anything at the time, but I remember thinking, *'When I wake up, I'm going to feel terrible,'* and of course I did, plus nursing a bright purple bruise on my chin.

Also, the guy I was seeing at the time wasn't happy with my behaviour. He didn't directly tell me, but in the morning, he said he needed to go home as soon as he awoke. I immediately thought the worst and with my thumping headache started to catastrophise, *'What did I say? Who did I annoy? Is he going to break up with me because of my behaviour?'* More and more questions went around and round in my head. Of course, a few days after the party and seeing this behaviour, he soon ended the relationship.

I wasn't drinking when we first started going out. He was not a big drinker but encouraged me one Friday night to have a drink and I hesitated, as I knew I was having issues with alcohol at the time. We never really had anything in common and he didn't seem that interested in me at all. I remember when I had a car accident where a guy partly hit my car from behind while travelling 80 kph and veering over the median strip. The first place I wanted to go was my boyfriend's house and have a drink with him and relax and be comforted by him. I knocked on his front door and the first thing he said after I told him I had a car accident was, *'Why didn't you just go home, rather than coming here?'* I told him he was the first person I wanted to see after having my accident. I turned to leave and said, *'Don't worry, I'll just go home if you don't want me here.'* I turned away with tears welling up in my eyes, trying to not let him see how disappointed I was with his response. As I started walking away, he yelled, *'Come back, don't walk home, it's going to be dark soon.'* I breathed a sigh of relief, as it was going to take me at least 45 minutes to an hour to walk home. As I walked closer, I put my head down and wiped my tears away. He ushered me inside, then gave me a kiss on the cheek as I walked in. I simply couldn't understand why he didn't want to be with me. I ignored the fact that we did not have anything in common and he knew very little about me. Quite simply, the use of alcohol blinded me, and I could not see what was in front of me, in that it was contributing to my incompatible, failing relationships.

A year later when I was thirty-seven, I woke up one morning, after many nights in a row of heavy drinking, and opened one eyelid and looked over my bed. Books were sprawled everywhere, there were two empty red wine bottles on my bedside table. I had now resorted to drinking in my bedroom on my own every night. At the time I so desperately wanted to sleep again but my mind was going a hundred miles an hour. My mind started, *'You need to get up, you promised friends you would come over, who in the hell were you talking to on internet dating last night? What did you say?'* But then there was part of my brain that thought, *'You don't have to do anything, just stay here in bed.'* Catastrophising just became a part of my life and every morning after I drank (which was most days) I would be paranoid I had annoyed someone or said something ridiculous that I knew I would regret. My body ached and my head felt like it was in a pinball machine. Every time I moved it hurt. As I lifted my head, I looked down to realise I had passed out, and was still in last night's clothes.

I turned my head to the nearest bedside table and sculled the glass of water sitting there. I needed more. I pulled the doona off me and slowly dragged myself out of bed and walked to the laundry, which was right beside my bedroom. Filled my glass to the top where it almost overflowed and sculled another. I could not bear to drink more even though my body craved it. As I stood there my housemate rushed through the door with a washing basket tucked under his arm. *'Feeling a bit seedy today, are we?'* *'No comment,'* I replied sourly. I can't remember the time when I had become this grumpy, moody, horrible person in the morning. I hated myself for becoming this way. I would shudder every time something venomous came out of my mouth. I used to be a bright, bubbly person everyone hated to see in the morning because I was so chirpy! It was the daily drinking that was doing this to me. Feeling happy or down after work and drinking myself into oblivion and then getting up the next morning, going through the motions and then doing it all again the following night. Thoughts would go through my head in the morning, *'This has to stop! What are you doing?'* but then when I realised people either weren't annoyed at me or I hadn't offended anyone, it would get to the end of the workday and I would drink heavily once again.

Only a few weeks later I met a guy who was tall, dark and handsome, very charismatic and charming. He had a great sense of humour and I thought we had similar interests as we chatted for the first few hours, but all I was doing was agreeing with everything he was saying. At the time I thought I had met the love of my life, but all I was doing was being that chameleon again. I also discovered one massive problem — he was a big drinker. Of course, when he drank a lot, I drank a lot. We both became judgemental, he would often say he didn't like public displays of affection, which upset me, as I did. I would often catastrophise, *'Why is he embarrassed to be seen with me?'* *'What is wrong with me?'* Although

I spent a lot of time with him, the only way I got to know him was in the bedroom. The most we ever spoke was in the first few hours on our first date; other than that, we didn't really talk about anything of substance. I thought at the time that this was the best relationship and was thinking like a giddy teenager – liking someone based on looks alone. I thought I could get him to like me, but I was very wrong. Everyone kept telling me he was good looking, and I knew he was very easy on the eye, but who was I trying to prove that he was *the one* to, myself or my friends? Now I know all I was trying to prove to my friends was that I deserved to be with a good-looking guy.

He would often tell me I was a mess and I needed to control myself, but he always wanted to spend time with me. I was confused, he was giving me mixed messages. He wanted me, then he didn't and would say we weren't right together. He initiated contact by sending me messages when he was drunk and of course I read this as a sign that he liked me. Of course, as soon as he asked me to come over, I was getting ready, calling a cab, drinking heavily and in his bed a short time later. He was a complex character who was very difficult to work out and with me always being in a drunken stupor around him, I was never going to work him out. One night I was about to drive home drunk after a massive fight about how he was using me. Although he didn't treat me well and only used me when he needed me, I am thankful he stopped me from driving home that night.

It is common where people who have consumed alcohol in their life, will most likely have experienced a night where their behaviour was out of control – let their emotions take over, slept with the wrong person. I'm not suggesting this is everyone, but when it happens it's like you are living outside of your body, especially when you are really drunk.

I often questioned the morning after a big night, *'Who have I become?'* I wasn't the person my mum raised, and I wasn't the person I wanted to be. I was desperately longing for someone to love me, so I would do these weird and wonderful things to get what I wanted. I suppose I didn't know what I truly wanted, but I knew it wasn't me and little did I know I wasn't going to get love, if I was acting like the way I was. If a guy was lovely and was prepared to treat me like I wanted to be treated and wasn't drinking as much as me, I just thought they were boring. I sabotaged something good for my love of drinking. Unfortunately, I was one of those people who would take the bait of those that wanted to take advantage of me, because of having low self-esteem and just wanting someone, anyone, to like me. Of course, when there was someone who didn't appeal to what I wanted then I would use them, just to make myself feel better. Most of them ran, and ran fast! I would have the day-after regret and feel terribly guilty and then would do it all over again. I just wasn't learning from my mistakes and turning into a person I hated.

 Mary's wisdom for living an alcohol-free life

How can you do dating/relationships better?

Get to know the person before dating them – it's all too easy these days to chat to someone for two hours online (when drunk) and think you know everything about them and believe you are ready to go on a date. Try chatting to them for a few weeks (or longer) before you meet up with them. If they really want to get to know you, they won't mind.

If you decide to stop drinking, engage in an activity you used to enjoy – by doing this you are moving your focus away from the drinking onto your healthy activity. After a while, you may then realise you are now feeling more comfortable to date. If you're in a relationship, maybe you could engage in an activity with your partner.

Don't drink heavily when you go on a date for the first time – I couldn't count how many times I went on first dates and got absolutely plastered and turned the guy off for good! It is not a good introduction to who you are. You want to show them the best of you, not the worst!

Being different when drunk – displaying erratic and/or passive aggressive behaviour when with a current/potential partner is not an ingredient for a healthy relationship. From experience (and as you have read so far) this can only end in misery.

 Journal prompts...

- **Name three goals/strategies** you can set BEFORE you go on a date. For example, *Try setting yourself a goal when dating to only have one or two drinks, then go home on your own.*
    - Also, try not to then drink more when you get home as this could lead to further contact. Setting these goals before you go on the date can help plan your night out and be more prepared for what's to come.
- **Name three goals/strategies** to use when getting to know someone online/talking on the phone to ensure you are not jumping in too quickly. For example, *set yourself a goal of talking online for a month and then meeting them in person OR meeting someone out at a bar or at a party, deciding not to go home with them but instead getting to know them first.*
- **List four alcohol-free activities** can you engage with, so dating/your relationship is not your sole focus. For example, *painting, regularly catching up with a friend for a walk followed by a coffee.*

- **What are four non-alcohol related questions** you could ask your partner/date? For example, *Partner – What's one thing about yourself you've never told me? Date – Where did you grow up? Is there a type of food you hate?*
- **What goes through your mind** before you come home from a night out with your partner/date? List four things that immediately enter your mind.
  – **Now write down two alternatives** not related to drinking.

Dating and Relationships

Chapter 9
When drinking starts to affect work

'The guilt and shame of what I could remember that I'd done was huge. For hours I thought about who I might have offended and how sick I felt. It wasn't me; it was the alcohol.'
Mary Stuart

I have high expectations for myself and always have done since I was young; always wanting to do the right thing both in my personal and work life. At thirty-eight, my drinking was so bad, and I drank so much during the evenings, I used to walk into work thinking, *'Can they smell the alcohol?'* I would feel dread and shame in the pit of my stomach. A feeling that at any time I was going to get into trouble. Even knowing this I continued to do it over and over, and over again. The addiction was definitely taking over. The after-work celebration (or commiseration) of going to the bottle shop and getting two bottles, sometimes three, to get my fix. My mind was always thinking, especially when I was drinking.... *how much can I get away with?* I was never a risk taker, so I was confused by why I thought like this. The mornings after though, that's when the real me took over — the guilt and shame of what I could remember I'd done. For hours I thought about who I might have offended and how sick I felt. It wasn't me; it was the alcohol. I thought I was invincible there for a while and could get away with most things. *'What had I become? Where did the person I used to be disappear to?'* I don't think I can remember when the crossover from being a nice, respectable girl that got drunk to have fun, to this horrible person who would do and say anything when drunk, happened. Surprisingly, this is not when my drinking was actually at its worst.

There was one time I had agreed to do a speech for an anniversary work event. I woke up that morning with my hands shaking uncontrollably. There had been other mornings when this had happened, but this day was an exceptionally bad day. I was starting to get alcohol withdrawals. The World Health Organisation (WHO)[4] states some of the symptoms associated with this are a fast heart rate, tremors (which is what I had), anxiety (definitely had this and had done since I was a child), sickness, insomnia, irritability, seizures or shallow breathing.

I turned up to work and before the time of the speech, I sat at my desk to ensure people wouldn't notice that I was shaking. I briefly spoke with my manager and she asked me about the speech and whether I was ready. I sat on my hands and said, *'I'm ready, it's all good.'* She smiled and walked away. I felt sick, I had nothing in my stomach and there was only half an hour before I was due to speak. I prepared a semi structured speech and I waited for my manager to speak. I moved around in my seat as though I was nervous and all of her words went straight over my

---

4. https://www.who.int/substance_abuse/terminology/withdrawal/en/

head because all I could think was, *'How am I going to do this without making it obvious I'm shaking?'* I then heard, *'Thank you... Mary would you like to come up?'* I slowly walked to the front of the room. I started my speech, thanking people for coming and I had my notes written on an A4 piece of paper. Every time I looked at the page it was shaking from my hands underneath. People just thought I was nervous, but I was uncontrollably shaking which meant that the alcohol was taking over. One of my colleagues came up to me later and praised me for a good speech, asking, *'Were you nervous, as you were shaking quite a lot?'* I replied, *'Yeah I was nervous, but the shaking just made me get in my own head.'*

Alcohol Think Again is a public education campaign in Western Australia[5] where they state that quite often, we believe after a big night we're fine when we wake to go to work. However, the use of alcohol soon becomes an occupational health and safety issue where we might still be intoxicated or hungover, where we are not giving our best work performance.

I remember having a really bad day at work once and coming home and having three large glasses of wine in quick succession, not realising that I still needed to take calls for work. I was mortified when the phone rang, and I knew I had to answer it. I composed myself and answered the phone. Luckily, it was someone from a service provider I knew and the phone call was going to be quick. *'Hi Mary, I just wanted to let you know I have moved a client's service delivery time to 2 p.m., is that okay? I've already spoken with the client.'* I said, *'Sure, no problem. Have a good night.'* I made a note on the client's file and thought, *'Surely you slurred your words, and what if they realised you had been drinking?'*

---

5. https://alcoholthinkagain.com.au/alcohol-your-community/alcohol-the-workplace/

This terrifying, catastrophising voice went on for a few minutes until I told myself internally, I can't do anything about it now. However, I really was worried, so I kept drinking, so I would completely forget about it. After that, I stared at the phone and hoped it didn't ring again and luckily it didn't. I was living on the edge and knowing I could possibly get in trouble for this but took the risk anyway. The horrible day I had, had well and truly taken over in my mind. I had soon forgotten about the call and everything else that occurred that day and continued to drink, once again thinking everything would just go away and get better.

I received a call about a week and a half later while I was driving back from interstate for work. It was my manager, asking if I had been drinking one night while I was taking after hours calls and quite honestly, I said, *'Not that I can remember.'* I seriously could not remember. She then changed the tone of her voice and it became much more serious. *'I have spoken with one of our service providers and they told me that they spoke with you a couple of weeks ago and you sounded intoxicated. Can you tell me what happened?'* I went silent on the other end of the phone; it all came back to me and all of the colour drained from my face. I then 'fessed up and said, *'I'm really sorry, I had forgotten I was on call that evening and I had a really bad day at work that day and just wanted to come home and have a glass of wine.'* She sighed heavily and said, *'I know you are always normally so reliable and such a good worker, so I just want you to think before you get home next time to ensure you remember you are on call. Please do not do it again, I won't be so lenient next time. Take this as an informal warning.'* I was so ashamed and embarrassed. I just felt terrible. I had never before been given a warning for anything at work. I always prided myself on my integrity and strong work ethic and now I really couldn't. What had I become? The sad thing was, while I was talking to my manager, I was nursing a hangover.

I was living in this constant shame and embarrassment, but I continued to drink as my body craved it during the day, and especially at the end of a workday. I would daydream of being at home relaxing and thinking about a glass of wine in my hand, the sensation of wine making my body warm from the inside out. That feeling I would have of blocking out my stressful workday was (at the time) the best feeling in the world and I wanted more of it.

Alcohol slows down and decreases your performance with work or study, and it can also have a significant impact on your relationships.

 Mary's wisdom for living an alcohol-free life

Analyse your productivity at work – Have you or your boss noticed a drop in your productivity? If so, work out where it has dropped and go back to the strategies that worked before your drinking affected your work performance.

Find out if your workplace has support services – most workplaces have an Employment Assistance Program (counselling service) and decide if you want to use this service (normally confidential). If they do not provide this support, you may want to consider external support (Go to Journal prompts in Chapter 7).

Determine if you feel comfortable enough telling your boss to enlist further support – attempt to sit down with your boss (if you feel comfortable) to ask for support in your productivity. Suggest some accountability measures around supervision and that you require it to be more often so you can go over your work to ensure it is up to standard. This way it can be about your work and not about your drinking.

Stressors will always be a part of life – We all have things happen in our lives but that is no excuse to pick up a bottle. This can actually make us feel so much worse, not only about the situation but other stressful things that happen in life, day to day.

 Journal prompts...

- **What goes through your mind** before you come home from work? List four things that immediately enter you mind. Now think of two alternatives not related to drinking.
- Go through your current physical after-work rituals. For example, *I pack my desk up, say a brief goodbye to everyone, walk the same way home, past the bottle shop, grab two to three bottles of wine, then walk home.*
    - Now list four things you can do differently to change the way you think as you leave work. For example, *I pack my desk up, then ensure I chat to one person to ask how their day was, walk a different route home, in the opposite direction to the bottle shop, grab my bike and go for a ride for half an hour.*
- **What can you improve** upon when it comes to your work productivity? List four things that worked before your drinking got out of control.
- **What would you like** your work like to look like?
    - What are your career goals? Does that involve staying in the same job or changing careers altogether?
- **When do you begin thinking** about alcohol during the day? Monitor this for one week to see if there is a pattern emerging. If so, change your rituals at that time of the day (use the first two points in this Chapter's Journal prompts to do this, except change it to that time of the day)
    - If it is while you are at work, how does it affect your work performance?

When drinking starts to affect work

When drinking starts to affect work

Chapter 10
Second attempt... or was it?

'I even bought a bike and was riding around the park every morning in the crisp winter chill, I enjoyed the cold breeze rushing past my cheeks and just thought how fresh and healthy I felt.'
Mary Stuart

I was thirty-nine when I decided to go alcohol-free for the second time. I was walking home from work one night; it was cold and drizzly, the rain was targeting my face and my breathing was laboured. I still felt really bad from drinking the night before. I thought to myself, *'This has to stop!'* I got to the back door of my apartment which was undercover, but the wind nevertheless managed to swirl around in the U-shaped little nook in between my neighbour's entry and my apartment door. As I opened the door the wind pushed against the wall and I quickly walked around and struggled to push it closed. As I took a deep breath I thought, *'Thank god I'm inside.'* Just the small five-minute walk from work was now an effort and I knew my drinking was out of control.

Normally, as soon as I walked in the door, I would have been pouring myself a large glass of wine and either watched trashy, mind-numbing shows on TV or listened to music and sang my lungs out, or cried, depending on what song it was. However, tonight I wanted to do something different. I walked into my bedroom and opened my large wardrobe cupboard, reached to the top shelf and pulled out my sketch book and graphite pencils. I spent the remainder of the night sketching and thinking about what I was going to paint on a canvas, which I had shoved to the back of the wardrobe months ago when I moved in. You see, my drinking pushed all the activities I was interested in and good at, to the side. Yes, I decided to go cold turkey from that day onwards, but unbeknownst to me things would start to get better. I was about to meet my second husband.

I was living on my own for the first time. I even bought a bike and was riding around the park every morning in the crisp winter chill. I enjoyed the cold breeze rushing past my cheeks and just thought how fresh and healthy I felt. My motivation for quitting at the time was simply that I was struggling to pay the rent on my beautiful apartment working two jobs and spending most of my money on alcohol and having nothing to show for it.

I was a month into my alcohol-free life, and it was going very well. I was also back on internet dating after a two-month break. I thought maybe I could meet someone who also didn't drink or only drank on the odd occasion. A guy sent me a message without a photo and wanted to chat. I declined, not knowing who this person was, as it was usually the guys who were, as my mum would say, *'Only after one thing'* who usually didn't have a photo. He then sent me a written message and I rolled my eyes, thinking, *'This guy just isn't giving up!'* Once I realised it was Paul, an old friend (who I secretly liked in high school – and the guy I earlier tried to kiss in the nightclub) I was very happy. In high school he had given me two beautiful Swarovski crystals that I had kept for so long, until I had moved to this apartment, when they had disappeared. I felt like this was fate; I was meant to be in contact with him at this point, not drinking and feeling like my life was back on track.

Paul asked in a message if I wanted to talk over the phone, so I gave him my number and he called. His voice sounded like he was unwell, but he said his voice was permanently that way due to an accident. He asked if I wanted to meet up and I said yes, but I was nervously worried he would be different to what I had remembered, not because of his voice, but I just thought he wouldn't be the guy I fell for in high school. I'm sure he was nervous, just like I was. I asked him if he wanted to meet at a café in a suburb north of Melbourne. He warned me he may not be able to talk much as it would be loud, but I said I didn't mind, and it would just be nice to see him.

When I got there, I saw him and my jaw dropped as I thought, *'He is still as handsome as ever without hair!'* I loved the new look! I was very happy to see him, but I wanted to play it cool and not be overly excited, even though inside I was. We spoke for hours and enjoyed pizza and pasta. His voice failed him a few times, so he grabbed a pen and paper and wrote down what he wanted to say. It was just refreshing to go out with him, not drink and just enjoy his company. It helped that I knew him and that we had so much to catch up on.

We spent the whole day together talking about what we had been up to over the past 20-plus years. I spoke about my marriage and how it didn't work out, he said the same. It was very surprising that we'd had similar experiences, it was like we had married the same person. We were both enjoying ourselves so much, we walked out of the restaurant and he turned to me and said, *'Would you like to do something else? I'm not ready to go home just yet.'* I smiled at him and excitedly said, *'Me neither!'* We then walked to the cinemas on the same street which wasn't showing the movie we wanted to see, so we got into the car, looked at each other, leaned in and he lightly kissed me on the lips. Paul then calmly said, *'So would you like to find another cinema to go to?'. 'Sure!'* I replied, as I turned to him and smiled.

As we walked, we talked and talked, very different from when he used to drive me home from school in his gun-metal grey Holden Gemini, where we would both say absolutely nothing and sit there twitching with nervous energy. I wasn't sure he liked me, but then again, I sort of knew he did from the things he used to do for me. In high school he was definitely a guy I wanted to know more. I was very happy, knowing that he was now finally letting me in.

We never left each other's side from that day on. Things were going so great he asked if I would go with him to Spain in September of the same year. All of a sudden, we were jetting off to Spain. As we boarded the plane I turned and said to Paul *'Have a guess what?! I think I might have a red wine to celebrate our first trip together.'* He then said, *'Why not?'* We both had a couple of drinks and what happened? I had the bug again. One touch of alcohol on the lips and I was gone! We drank every day of the two weeks we were there. I was hooked again. Although it was all out of happiness, and it being the best holiday I had ever been on, I was drunk every day! Back to feeling like rubbish every morning. We came back from Spain and I continued to drink like I used to. It was a clear indicator that I wasn't the *cut down, only drink on holidays* type of person. This alcohol-free stint had only been just under four months. The longest period I had been alcohol-free.

Mary's wisdom for living an alcohol-free life

You've stopped being involved in anything that used to interest you – this is when drinking becomes your biggest pastime. Your partner/friends/family will start to see you have a better relationship with the bottle and will walk if you don't make steps to resolve the issue. Start engaging in an activity you used to love. You will soon swap drinking for the new activity.

Don't put pressure on yourself if you fail the first or even second time – get back on the horse and ride! Remember, it took me three attempts before I finally settled on an alcohol-free life, on the fourth try. Remember, if you slip up, there is no point focusing on the past. Always move forward!

Learn from your mistakes – Use what you have written in your journal to learn what you learned from this alcohol-free period. As previously stated, don't beat yourself up. Learn and move on.

Don't be so hard on yourself – I am a perfectionist, and I would (and sometimes still) beat myself up that I wasn't more determined and that I failed. Always remember, it is not failure, it's a learning opportunity. Reward yourself for giving it a go. Buy yourself a small gift – NOT ALCOHOL! And remind yourself you can do it again.

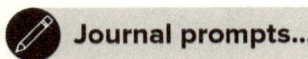

Journal prompts...

This is now an opportunity to look at your drinking habits

- **Look at the positives and negatives of drinking.** Draw a line down the centre of a page in your journal. Write positives on one side and negatives on the other. Then write the positives of drinking, then repeat but now write the negatives. Choose three negatives above (that stand out to you):
  - What about each one do you see as negative?
  - How has each one negatively impacted your life?
- **List four questions** you can ask yourself about your drinking without using *why* and instead use *when, where, what* and *how*.
  - For example, *How much do I drink? When do I drink the most? What am I like when I drink? Where are the places I tend to drink the most?*
  - Now answer the questions you have written down.
- **If you have quit drinking before, list three things you learned** from that experience and list three things you would do differently next time. Remember it doesn't have to be something big.
- **What do I say to yourself** when you are about to have another drink?
  - Is it positive or negative? For example, *are you telling yourself not to have another drink or are you looking forward to another drink?*
- **When do I most often** find I drink to excess? For example, *weekends, after work drinks, Sunday afternoon?* Excess means different things to different people.
  - What is **your** excess? For example, *four bottles of wine a night is your excess*

Second attempt... or was it?

Living an Alcohol-free Life YOUR Way

Second attempt... or was it?

Chapter 11
Alcohol and disease

'I believe that my coeliac gene was triggered later in life as I drank way too much.'
Mary Stuart

Even though Paul and I were extremely happy, I continued to drink for the next few years. My Team Leader role for a not-for-profit organisation was wearing me down at the time and I was under the illusion that alcohol was getting me through my stressful work days. I had been diagnosed with Coeliac Disease in my early forties, after years of itchy skin and being tired, lethargic, pale as a ghost and just overall feeling terrible on a daily basis. I have now realised a lot of my problems related to alcohol and the gallons and (not just litres) I was consuming for so, so long.

According to Coeliac Australia[6], Coeliac Disease causes damage to the bowel where someone with Coeliac Disease ingests gluten, which causes the malabsorption of food and drink. The small hair like protrusions in the stomach called villi, are damaged which causes the malabsorption.

In my case of my high alcohol consumption, I believed, based on what I had learned about Coeliac Disease, once I was diagnosed and continued to drink heavily, I was at a higher risk of developing physical dependence. It made sense; if I was drinking as much as I was and not eating gluten, it was likely I was absorbing greater amounts of alcohol into my gut quicker.

Although I can't be sure, I believe that my coeliac gene was triggered later in life as I drank way too much. Although I was diagnosed in my early forties, but I knew there was something wrong way before this. I was going to my family doctor telling him I had itchy skin, diarrhea, I was exhausted all the time and he just thought it was a skin allergy. After spending thousands of dollars on specialist appointments, when Paul and I decided to move to regional Victoria a few years later, it was then I was diagnosed with Coeliac Disease. I was relieved to finally know what was wrong with me. I was going through life thinking those ailments were my *normal*, only running on a small amount of fuel, but I was so wrong.

I thought I would research the Paleo diet, to see if it would make me feel better. Having fresh, organic ingredients, and drinking Kombucha daily seemed like a wonderful idea, to get everything back on track. For the first eight months (of the sixteen months) on the diet, I continued to drink alcohol heavily until I realised, I wasn't losing any weight and I actually still felt terrible, waking up with hangovers every day. Just being on the diet and continuing to drink was not going to make anything better, so

---

6. https://www.coeliac.org.au/s/coeliac-disease

I knew I had to stop drinking once again. I also stopped being so strict with the Paleo diet but continued to follow it loosely, to what suited me at that time. It wasn't the diet; it was my drinking, it was affecting everything.

This was my third proper attempt at quitting booze, of course not counting the one or two days here and there thinking I was going to quit but never did. I wanted to continue with a healthy diet, eliminating sugar. I decided my diet and health was my next priority, so I researched Naturopaths to get my *balance* back. I was concerned I had put on so much weight and just wanted to feel healthier. The Paleo diet was helping very slowly but drinking for the first eight months didn't help at all. I decided *'that's it'* and just stopped drinking, not really thinking it through. Although I had learned a lot from my previous attempts, it wouldn't be until later when I realise taking those combined learnings forward would actually help me live an alcohol-free life for good!

 Mary's wisdom for living an alcohol-free life

Changing your diet for the long-term can assist with living an alcohol-free life – Consider adjusting your diet when you quit - you don't have to drastically change it like I did. I'm sure small changes such as eating a slightly healthier breakfast will assist in helping you feel better.

Exercise – Not only is exercise great for your mental health and a way to keep your mind off alcohol but it can get you into a different routine. Just remember, the longer you drink the worse the health issues.

Get a health check from your GP or visit a Naturopath – doesn't matter whether you're into traditional or alternative medicine, make sure your body is working the way it should be. Getting your health sorted will give you another focus to live an alcohol-free life.

> **If you do find out there is something wrong** – take the advice of your health professional and get on with your life. Of course, it is okay to get upset when you find out about disease or illness in your body. Being positive about the diagnosis can assist with you getting through when you're not feeling so well.

 Journal prompts...

- **Do you feel unwell?** For example, sore stomach, headaches, poor bowel movements.
    – If so, list two ailments you are experiencing.
- **When was the last time you saw a doctor** and received a full check-up?
- **How can you create more balance** in your life? List two things.
- **What are two positive goals** for your physical health? For example, *I would like to feel fresh five mornings per week – no fogginess.*

Note: when deciding on a goal, keep them small in the beginning and make them bigger as you start to get traction.

    – Do these goals balance with any other life goals you may have? If not, what can you do to be able to align your goals, so it is not so overwhelming? You want your goals to work alongside each other, otherwise it will be difficult to achieve. For example, *if one of your goals is going out with friends more and you also want to quit alcohol. Make sure your alcohol-free goals are realistic to sit alongside your 'going out' goal.*
- **How many hours of sleep** are you getting a night?
    – If under 8 hours a night, how can you improve this?

Alcohol and disease

Living an Alcohol-free Life YOUR Way

Alcohol and disease

Chapter 12
Stressful events and celebrations

'I continued to drink and felt like this was getting me through, but in fact it was making me feel worse.'
Mary Stuart

I will never forget the day when my mum found out she had cancer. It was February 2016 when my eldest brother, mum and I sat in our family doctor's office. Our doctor sat there facing all of us, then looked to the floor to compose himself before speaking. *'Well, we've had a look at your scan and unfortunately we have found a mass in your uterus and it's quite large. The likelihood is that it's uterine cancer, but we would need to get it looked at further at the Royal Women's hospital by an oncologist.'* I held mum's hand and she squeezed it, as she sobbed. I looked over at my brother as I saw tears rolling down his face. I tried to hold my tears in, but I couldn't help it, they fell quickly down my cheeks. I looked over at our family doctor and he also had tears rolling down his cheek. Wiping it away, he said to mum, *'I'm sorry this has happened to such a beautiful person.'* Mum asked if she was going to die and the doctor said, *'I think it is best for the oncologist to have a look and then we can talk about it further.'* Mum could see it on his face that it wasn't good — we all could. The timing was horrible as she was just about to have her 73rd birthday. All the emotions that come with a cherished family member finding out they have cancer are indescribable.

Paul and I had already set our wedding date for June that year and knew that we had to make the next few months special for my mum. Although I had good intentions on Mother's Day that year, I got terribly drunk and remember my mum saying to me, *'Why are you drinking so much?'* I remember turning to her and in my raised, drunk voice, *'Why do you think? My poor mum has cancer and there is nothing I can do.'* Although this may not seem that bad to you, to this day that conversation belts around in my head. *'How could I have spoken to her in that way when it was her that was going through it?'* I stopped drinking for a few days after that as I was so ashamed. At this point, it had been the longest period without alcohol — I quit in late 2015 and then drank on Mother's Day (May 2016). It had still not quite sunk in that my mum was unwell. Although she was tired a lot and was exhausted from all of her appointments and radiation sessions, she was still my lovable mum. She still enjoyed a laugh, still loved hearing our stories and got fired up when she was barracking for her beloved AFL football team, the Bombers.

The following month came, and with it my wedding day. My beautiful mum had made my dress, even though I kept saying to her it might be best for someone else to do it because she didn't feel one hundred percent. My mum made most of my clothes growing up, from pretty frilly dresses to end of school functions and bridesmaid's dresses. She wanted to make my wedding dress, as it could be the last dress she made for me.

Since we started planning our wedding, I planned not to drink alcohol on the day, however as the days got closer, I felt like a celebratory drink would be nice. It was a wonderful wedding day. My best friend and I drank champagne whilst we were getting ready in the morning. Only a few hours passed, and we had already gone through two bottles of champagne, just the two of us. I felt like I was in control for most of the day which felt good. Times like this used to play tricks with my mind where afterwards I would think I was fine, and that my drinking wasn't that bad. As I didn't feel out of control and was quite well behaved at our wedding reception, I continued to drink when we got home as we were opening all of our cards from the wishing well. I drank until I passed out.

Post-wedding celebrations, Paul would allow me to drink until I would fall asleep on the couch with Eddie, our dog. He would take funny photos of me and we would laugh it off in the morning, but he had to have been worried about my drinking. I definitely was. At this stage, I was drinking up to almost three bottles of wine a night! I had to be open and honest with him and tell him I was addicted to alcohol and there was no chance I could have a sip of alcohol without falling off the wagon.

There was one night where I yelled at him when I was really drunk. Paul and I never fought but he was so annoyed with me he stormed off to bed. I woke the next morning, felt like my body was about to shut down. I snuck out to the bedroom while Paul was still sleeping. With my head lowered I walked out into the back garden to water the vegetable patch. Every so often I turned back to the house to see if he had woken. I wanted to talk with him. My catastrophising was going crazy, *'What if he no longer loves me? What if I need to leave? What if he no longer wants to stay?'* I wanted to let him know how much I was struggling with my addiction. The last time I turned he slowly walked over, taking each step off the veranda, as soon as he got closer, I started sobbing. He opened his arms, and I tucked my head into his chest and then I cried, *'I'm so sorry, I don't know what's wrong with me. I need to stop drinking. I have a problem.'* As he squeezed me, he said, *'It's okay my love, it's not that bad, you just get a little silly when you've had too much, and you want to try and fight with me.'* I lifted my head to look at him. *'Oh but it is that bad; I have an addiction, my love,'* I said, tucking my head back into his chest. I couldn't see his face at that point, but I'm sure he had a worried look on his face.

He thought he was helping me by going out to buy more wine when I was stressed from work and also thinking I enjoyed wine after work; however, this was only enabling me. He knows that now. He really thought I enjoyed drinking, but I was addicted. There was no way I was going to lose my beautiful, caring, loving man to alcohol.

 Mary's wisdom for living an alcohol-free life

Celebrations or commiserations were always an excuse to drink – It didn't matter whether I was happy or sad, I found an excuse to drink myself into oblivion. Once you have determined what triggers you to drink then you can create your own goals/strategies.

I remember I have been to plenty of events alcohol-free – Think about a time when you went to an event where you enjoyed yourself without alcohol – this could also be when you were younger. Adopt some strategies based on those events.

Having alternatives to just reaching for the bottle – For me, (as I previously mentioned) having other activities I was interested in (and still am) was so important to living an alcohol-free life. It's particular vital when stressful events arise. For me it was working out all of the reasons why I drank through journaling and discovering new things about myself on my alcohol-free journey.

Plan, plan, plan – Sometimes stressful or celebratory events happen unexpectedly! Doing some planning in advance means you won't get caught in a situation you don't want to be in.

 Journal prompts...

- **What are your triggers** when it comes to drinking?
  Answer Y (there is a trigger) or N (there is no trigger) to the following:
  - When someone offers you a drink? Y/N
  - Is it when you are stressed from work? Y/N
  - Any celebration? Y/N
  - Funerals? Y/N
  - Weddings? Y/N
  - Sitting at home on your own? Y/N
  - Seeing others drinking? Y/N
  - Simply seeing alcohol bottles? Y/N
  - Driving/walking past the bottle shop? Y/N

  What about the triggers you answered yes to, make them triggers for you?
- **List two major events** that have affected you negatively over the past two years:
  - How did you cope?
  - If one of those coping strategies was to drink, what can you do differently to cope?
- **List two major events** that have affected you positively over the past two years:
  - How did you celebrate?

- If you drank, what can you do differently to celebrate? List three non-drinking related alternatives.
- **With the alternatives** you have listed above, what can you implement right now?
- **Write a plan** for when those unexpected events are thrust upon you.
  - What do you say?
  - What does your body language look like?
  - What would you do for a stressful event as opposed to a celebratory event?

Stressful events and celebrations

Living an Alcohol-free Life YOUR Way

Stressful events and celebrations

Chapter 13
Living an alcohol-free life

*'I remember being on the phone with an old friend and they said they could barely understand me because I was so drunk. I got angry with them and hung up.
I woke the next morning ashamed of myself.'*
Mary Stuart

In early 2017 my mum felt as though she was getting the flu and couldn't breathe very well. My brother called an ambulance and told us to meet him at the hospital. Here was where we were told my mum had stage four cancer. I remember looking at my brother across the room as he broke down and cried. I could no longer hold it in. I was holding my mum's hand. I squeezed it and put my head down and cried. I looked up and mum was looking at me and she gave my hand a little shake (as she often did) and said encouragingly, *'C'mon, don't get upset, 'cause you will make me upset.'* I knew what the oncologist was saying, but I don't think mum did. She looked at the oncologist as they spoke, afterwards she nodded and pretended to understand what they were saying, then she looked at me and asked, *'What does that mean?'* I lowered my head then looked her in the eyes, *'It's not good, mama.'* She broke down and cried. My brother walked over to her and rubbed her on the back as she cried harder. We thought the radiation was working and she was feeling a lot better apart from these 'flu-like' symptoms.

I continued to drink and felt like this was getting me through, but in fact it was making me feel worse. This continued until early November and my drinking was getting worse and worse. I was working with offenders in my job at the time and it was extremely stressful. I remember being on the phone one night after work with an old friend and they said they could barely understand me because I was so drunk. I got angry with them and hung up. I woke the next morning ashamed of myself. It was getting to the point where I was indecipherable, which was concerning as I felt as though maybe my brain was now being affected.

It was mid-November 2017, and I was scrolling through social media when I came across a few different videos about quitting drinking. Some of the phrases being used like *'alcohol is not the joy juice we think it is'* and *'alcohol promised so much but never delivered'* really resonated with me. I knew I wanted to quit this time, but I had to do something different to what I had done before. I decided to journal my feelings when I was drinking; both before I drank and when I had a hangover. I did this for 40 days while I was still drinking. I would randomly read over the pages I had written, to get myself in a headspace where I was simply disgusted with so many things I'd said and done. Reading things like: losing myself in alcohol, people I was hurting, quality time with my loved ones, the moodiness, the anxiety I was feeling, the list just went on and on.

Living an alcohol-free life

On Christmas Day 2017, I drank to excess and ate a fantastically cooked meal at my brother and sister-in-law's place. I enjoyed the day with my mum as I thought it may be the last Christmas I would spend with her. I woke the next day and went to write another entry in my diary and something made me want to read all of my journal entries from start to finish. Once I had finished, I felt sick to my stomach. I realised I was ready to quit. December 26, 2017 was to be the first day of my alcohol-free life. To keep me on track I decided to take one selfie every day, for 100 days. To make myself accountable, I posted one a day for the first 20 days on social media, then (so I wasn't boring everyone) posted every 10 days after that, so 30, 40, 50 etc. until I reached 100. I was getting praise, likes and so much love from everyone, it encouraged me to continue. Most of all, my mum was so proud of me. I continued until 120 days and then it just became a way of life. I had also learned from all of the previous occasions I quit alcohol. Yes, there were days I wanted to drink, and I had cold sweats at night, but I knew from the previous times that this would be over soon. The selfies showed me just how far I had come. I had colour in my face, my eyes were brighter and overall, I felt fantastic, so much so I wondered why I had let myself drink for so long.

I was around four months into my alcohol-free life when I came across an app called *I am Sober*, which I started using as I did have a few days and weeks where it was hard watching people drink or being out with people who drank. I entered my first day alcohol-free which was 26 December 2017 and watched the days go by. I now had my journal, my mum, my books, and social media to keep me on track. Initially I watched the app regularly and was chuffed at how well I was doing. Reading alcohol-free memoirs regularly before bed and contributing to social media groups really inspired me to continue on my journey over the next few months until I reached a point where I did not feel like I needed to be so involved. I also found as I started to get better I'd respond differently to reading a post where someone was struggling or I saw posts of people drinking non-alcoholic drinks out of bottles that looked like alcoholic drinks. In the early days, it triggered me. My strategy was to focus on the things that worked and to move away from those things that triggered me, in particular, if they were no longer serving me.

Paul is the most beautiful man I have ever met, so loving, caring, and always looking out for me. I love him so much and am so happy we found each other again. I've spoken openly to Paul about my drinking and he has been open and honest about when he was concerned about my drinking. He makes me feel good about myself and I have now (after a lot of work) switched back to the person I was in my early adult years, only I now have REAL confidence. Drinking heavily made me feel invisible for so long and feeling uncomfortable around the people I wanted to be around. I never thought I would get back to this point and I am so glad I did. I make sure I am enjoying what I am doing. I am truly enjoying my artwork at the moment. I have a thirst for it again. I am so grateful I have got to this point where alcohol is not controlling my life.

 Mary's wisdom for living an alcohol-free life

Focusing on the positive things you have done so far to keep you going – Looking over your selfies you've taken and looking back over how alcohol has made you feel in your journal keeps you on track. It will reinforce why you decided to quit.

Go to bed early and read something alcohol-free related before bed – Purchase a memoir, self-help book focused on being alcohol-free and read before bed. It will not only help you on track, but it will help you go to sleep. Getting enough sleep will help keep you feeling fresh, which is key to staying on track.

Continue to strengthen your mind around alcohol and what it does to your body – do some research about alcohol. For me I read and read and read so many alcohol-free related books and most of them, if not all, mentioned how bad alcohol was for my body. I held onto those thoughts and thought about this during the early stages of living alcohol-free. This is one of the useful things that has got me to where I am today.

Link with social media alcohol-free groups for support and read what other people are going through. If this is a trigger for you, then maybe organise to speak with someone face to face.

 Journal prompts...

- **What are four things** you can do to create a negative association with alcohol? For example, *think about rotten hangovers, think about my foggy head, think about how I was doing a half-hearted job at work because of my rotten hangovers.*
- **How did alcohol** make you feel, think, and do things that were embarrassing? Write four examples.
- Think about two reasons why you drank. For example, *it could be out of habit.*
- **List four things** you believe has been impacted by your drinking. For example, *cognition or your friendships/relationship.*
- **Take a selfie** of yourself for the first 40 days. Keep looking back at the Day 1 photo and write a description, if any, of the following changes:

- your skin
- pores
- hair
- eyes
- the shape of your face

** **If you feel confident, post your photos to social media or start sharing your photos with friends and family. This may just give you the accountability you need to continue.**

Living an alcohol-free life

Living an Alcohol-free Life YOUR Way

Living an alcohol-free life

Chapter 14

Staying on track (even when life throws things at you)

'This is all I was ever truly looking for in my life: happiness and the love of my family and friends.'
Mary Stuart

My mum was getting increasingly unwell and my drive for staying alcohol-free was stronger and stronger. I was becoming healthier and my drive was to be there for my mum even though I was living an hour away from her. I spent hours sitting on her bed, crying, and played songs she liked and we talked about how she would like her funeral to be. *'So mum, what do you want your funeral to look like?'* I said, as my eyes welled up. *'Oh, I want colourful roses on my coffin, and I want my favourite songs, like that Frank Sinatra song. I heard it on the radio at night... I want that,'* she said, so matter of fact. I felt like my mum knew it wasn't long before she left us, so it wasn't as upsetting for her. Of course, she had her moments where she was sad but nothing like when we were younger. I'm not going to lie, there were moments I thought of having a drink during these tough times. However, thinking about my mum and how much she needed me at this time, plus the negative associations I had created in my mind helped. My mum kept me on track with my drinking, as this time was all about her. I consistently read my journal, affirmed to myself why I wasn't drinking and how far I've come and how proud mum was of me.

My mum became even more unwell just before Christmas of 2018 and was in hospital having another bout of radiation. Drinking was the one thing furthest from my mind when she was really ill. My mum was always on my mind and I was worrying if she would make it to Christmas. We all had our fingers crossed she would be okay. I kept on track with my drinking as I was focused on mum.

In mid-March of 2019, I was just about to get ready for my husband's father's funeral, when I received a phone call from my brother. He was upset and as he sniffed, *'Mum's had a stroke and she's been taken in an ambulance.'* I quickly hung up from him and rushed around in what seemed like circles and sobbed, my head falling into my hands. Paul grabbed me and pulled me in as he hugged me. As my head was tucked into his chest I said in muffled sobs, *'Mum's had a stroke.'* Paul sighed and started crying. He then went into organisation mode and began to get things together and asked me if I could get into the shower, so we could get to the hospital before his dad's funeral. Although he was experiencing his own tragedy, he still wanted to be there for me.

Mum quickly went into the stroke ward and only two weeks later ended up in the palliative ward. Both of my brothers, plus Paul and I stood around her bed. The palliative doctor came in and explained what would happen to her, as he did not believe it would be long before she was gone. My brothers found it difficult to see her in this way and I said it was fine for them to leave if they wanted to. As Paul and I sat next to her, we were occasionally wetting her lips and the inside of her mouth with a large cotton tip. Paul eventually had to go and let our dog out of the house and wanted to make sure it was okay for him to leave. I calmly told him it was fine. As he kissed me on the forehead, a tear rolled down my cheek as I looked at my lovely mama. I stared at her, looking at how frail she had become, her lips dry and cracked and her eyes closed, breathing laboured, occasionally gasping and gurgling – just like the doctor had told us. I whispered, *'It's okay mama, when you are ready to go, you just go.'* It was only a few minutes after Paul left the room and not even an hour since my brothers had left, that she took her last breath. There were two conflicting things going through my head; I was happy she was not longer in pain, but I also didn't want her to leave. I paced around the room until someone came in and kept looking over at her wondering if she was really gone. I called Paul and sobbed, *'She's gone, my love.'*

In the past an event like this would have tipped me over the edge and felt like alcohol would have been the only thing to make me feel better. I know now alcohol never makes anything better.

Alcohol was the last thing on my mind on the day of her funeral. I just missed my mum and from that point, I drew on the strength and pride from my mum and knew I had to stay on the alcohol-free track. As the hearse drove away, I watched the colourful roses bobbling away in the back as they played the Bombers theme song, her favourite football team. I smiled and was so proud of everyone who had ensured she was able to have the beautiful send-off that we talked about.

At Christmas in 2019, my two brothers, my sister-in-law, her mum and Paul all gathered at a hotel in the city, the first Christmas without mum.

I suggested having it somewhere where my brother and sister-in-law didn't have to cook or clean, but it just wasn't the same without mum, and the dogs running around looking for scraps of food. In saying that, we had a lovely time together, joking about how much food we had gorged from the buffet. It was also the first time my extremely hospitable sister-in-law didn't ask if I wanted a glass of wine. Everyone was now just used to me not drinking and it felt good. I look down at my glass of soda water, then around the table where I got big smiles from everyone. I grinned and was so proud of myself and how far I had come. This is all I was ever truly looking for in my life; happiness and the love of my family and friends.

In 2021 as I write this, I am just celebrating my three year alcohol-free anniversary. Yes, I still catastrophise. Yes, I still have mild anxiety and the insecurities bubble to the surface every now and again, but I always go back to the way I now feel about alcohol. I am positive, if I had continued to lead an alcohol-fuelled life, my life would be very different. I'm sure I wouldn't be married to my beautiful husband and have such wonderfully supportive family and friends. As I head into my 50s (a few years off yet!), I have realised a few things:

- I am naturally an introvert but enjoy quality time with my wonderful friends and family.
- The whole time I was drinking I realised I disliked going out in large groups of people, but never really knew why. Knowing my personality, I am better in smaller groups or simply one-on-one.
- I am comfortable being myself and being alcohol-free; I make no apologies.
- I say no to things I don't feel comfortable doing.
- Alcohol is a poison, and I am healthier and happier without it.
- I am no longer wasting time, nursing hangovers, being grumpy or waiting to have my next drink.

- I spend time thinking about what I wrote in my journal to keep me on track.
- I'm doing the things I enjoy in life and making the most of my days rather than letting them waste away.

 Mary's wisdom for living an alcohol-free life

Alcohol will not solve your problems – I have learned over time that alcohol does not fix anything you are going through. Best to solve your problems in a healthier way.

The cycle of drinking, waking with a hangover and doing it all again will not help you cope with stressful events.

Don't wait until you lose someone or experience a stressful event before you decide to quit – Going through my mum's illness and death was definitely something which actually kept me on track rather than making me drink. It was due to the work I had done previously, however, that ensured I was strong enough to cope during stressful times.

Journaling before and after you drink but most of all read what you have written – I journaled for months and months. It was so useful to work out those small things that used to pass me by. *Do I twitch before I go out? Do I get grumpy knowing I have to go out?* Describing how all of those things felt to me were so important, so I could go back over them and read them again to remind myself how I actually felt.

 **Journal prompts...**

Only one last journal entry to go...

- **What are four positive steps** you can take in the future when something bad happens while you are alcohol-free?
- **What is your plan** over the next 30 days to maintain your alcohol-free life?
- **Now think about the next 6 – 12 months**, what is your plan?
- **What are four feelings** you haven't felt in a long time that you miss?
  - What can you do to get that feeling back again?
- **What is the reason why** you want to stay alcohol-free? Have a look back through your journal.
  - What stands out to you?
  - Assessing what you have written, what are you going to hold onto to motivate you to stay on track? For example, *you may have written a negative description of your association with alcohol.*

Staying on track (even when life throws things at you)

Staying on track (even when life throws things at you)

Final Message

I hope you will join me in experiencing the joys of an alcohol-free life. The time you get back, the quality time you get to spend with your loved ones, without the moodiness, the fear and insecurities. Instead of whatever is buzzing around in your head, why not replace it with thoughts of good things that are happening in your life rather than drinking. We owe it to the people we love to step up and be the person you always knew you were. It's not easy but it's completely bloody worth it!

What are you waiting for?

Mary xx

References

Alcohol Think Again website
https://alcoholthinkagain.com.au/alcohol-your-community/alcohol-the-workplace/

Australian Institute of Health and Welfare website
https://www.aihw.gov.au/reports/alcohol/alcohol-tobacco-other-drugs-australia/contents/drug-types/alcohol

Coeliac Disease Australia website
https://www.coeliac.org.au/s/coeliac-disease

Medical News Today website
https://www.medicalnewstoday.com/articles/320844#causes

World Health Organisation website
https://www.who.int/news-room/fact-sheets/detail/alcohol
https://www.who.int/substance_abuse/terminology/withdrawal/en/

www.ingramcontent.com/pod-product-compliance
Lightning Source LLC
Chambersburg PA
CBHW021953290426
44108CB00012B/1057